What People Are Saying About C

"Eye opening, thought provoking, and l...
of living out Hope in the midst of change
—**Lorilee Sheviak**, counselor, Grace Min...

"Author Ginger Harrington is the real deal. Her encouraging words always come wrapped in authenticity and love as she shares what she's learned from her own struggles. Her words are where I turn when I'm looking for a reminder of just how much God cares."
—**Edie Melson**, Director of Blue Ridge Mountain Christian Writers Conference

"Ginger Harrington is a writer who makes biblical principles applicable to everyday life. She writes as she lives—with grace, wisdom, authenticity, and an all-important dose of joy!"
—**Dr. Brenda Pace**, author of *Journey of a Military Wife*

"Ginger has a passion for the Word and for women who live the military family lifestyle. Her insight makes the road easier for those of us who face the regular challenges of loving those who serve. Her writing is a fresh breeze of renewal for all our Heroes at Home."
—**Ellie Kay**, founder of Heroes at Home

"Ginger Harrington's writing has changed my way of thinking about my relationship with God. She reminds me of the practical and fun ways that I can live out my life through Christ in me and how God desires to be in an intimate relationship with me. Her writing beckons me to accept my Savior's invitation to walk with Him daily—to worship Him in my everyday life and to dig into His word so I can go deeper."
—**Larissa Traquair**, Chief Inspirational Officer of the Grateful Tribe daily broadcast

"Transforming hearts and minds with God-centered wisdom, biblical truth, and realness, Ginger Harrington puts into words the many feelings and challenges that many of us face."
—**Salena Duffy**, Moms in Prayer International, Military Families Liaison

GINGER HARRINGTON

HOLY
IN THE
MOMENT

SIMPLE WAYS TO LOVE GOD

AND ENJOY YOUR LIFE

Abingdon Press
Nashville

HOLY IN THE MOMENT
SIMPLE WAYS TO LOVE GOD AND ENJOY YOUR LIFE
Copyright © 2018 by Virginia B. Harrington

All rights reserved.

Library of Congress Cataloging-in-Publication Data has been requested.

ISBN 978-1-5018-5780-5

Scripture quotations unless noted otherwise are taken from the New American Standard Bible® (NASB), Copyright © 1960, 1962, 1963, 1968, 1971, 1972, 1973, 1975, 1977, 1995 by The Lockman Foundation. Used by permission. www.Lockman.org

Scripture quotations marked MSG are taken from THE MESSAGE, copyright © 1993, 1994, 1995, 1996, 2000, 2001, 2002 by Eugene H. Peterson. Used by permission of NavPress. All rights reserved. Represented by Tyndale House Publishers, Inc.

Scripture quotations marked (NLT) are taken from the Holy Bible, New Living Translation, copyright © 1996, 2004, 2007, 2013, 2015 by Tyndale House Foundation. Used by permission of Tyndale House Publishers, Inc., Carol Stream, Illinois 60188. All rights reserved.

Scripture quotations marked (ESV) are taken from The Holy Bible, English Standard Version® (ESV®) Copyright © 2001 by Crossway, a publishing ministry of Good News Publishers. All rights reserved.

Scripture quotations marked (AMP) are taken from the Amplified® Bible (AMP), Copyright © 2015 by The Lockman Foundation. Used by permission. www.Lockman.org

Scripture quotations marked (NKJV) are taken from the New King James Version®. Copyright © 1982 by Thomas Nelson. Used by permission. All rights reserved.

Scripture quotations marked (TLB) are taken from The Living Bible copyright © 1971. Used by permission of Tyndale House Publishers, Inc., Carol Stream, Illinois 60188. All rights reserved.

Scripture quotations from The Authorized (King James) Version. Rights in the Authorized Version in the United Kingdom are vested in the Crown. Reproduced by permission of the Crown's patentee, Cambridge University Press.

Scripture quotations marked (NIV) are taken from the Holy Bible, New International Version®, NIV®. Copyright © 1973, 1978, 1984, 2011 by Biblica, Inc.™ Used by permission of Zondervan. All rights reserved worldwide. www.zondervan.com The "NIV" and "New International Version" are trademarks registered in the United States Patent and Trademark Office by Biblica, Inc.™

Scripture quotations marked HCSB®, are taken from the Holman Christian Standard Bible®, Copyright © 1999, 2000, 2002, 2003, 2009 by Holman Bible Publishers. Used by permission. HCSB® is a federally registered trademark of Holman Bible Publishers.

18 19 20 21 22 23 24 25 26—10 9 8 7 6 5 4 3 2 1
MANUFACTURED IN THE UNITED STATES OF AMERICA

CONTENTS

HOLY IN THE MOMENT

What difference is holiness making in your everyday life?

Does this question make you feel just a little uncomfortable? Yes, me too.

We know that we should be holy, but most of us don't feel holy. Confusing feelings with truth, it's easy to measure holiness based on what we do rather than on who we are in Christ. Not too long ago, when answering this question, I would have given you a list of all the ways I fall short, the mistakes I've made, and the many times I've struggled to trust God in the midst of uncertainty. To be honest, it was easier to view holiness as a spiritual concept rather than a practical way of living.

Heart, mind, soul, and strength—these are the gifts in our hands. Truth and Spirit, God comes alongside and we are no longer alone in the struggle. Added together, holy moments change lives from the inside out. This is a book about becoming aware of the power of sacred choices and good decisions made in the moment.

In this book you'll discover practical truths and simple ideas for godly living. How about you? Do you long to celebrate life with holy habits to impact your life both today and for eternity? Are you searching for ways to be more purposeful, to live well with sacred choices to

- love God and believe He is faithful?
- abide and rest in Christ?
- stop and pray?
- listen for God's guidance?
- embrace God's truth with obedience?

- spot faulty thinking based on lies you have believed?
- process feelings in a healthy way?
- enjoy life with good attitudes?
- love others well?
- invest in family and friends?
- rely on Christ as you work?

We will explore these questions in the pages of this book. Together, we'll discover that whole moments are for giving love—heart, soul, mind, and strength—to God, to others, and to ourselves. We'll practice choosing the one thing, *the best thing,* God asks of us. This is His way for the whole and the holy. The secret of living whole in this life is discovering the joy and freedom of God's grace filling all our days.

Today is our day to choose holiness. God's wholeness is a blessing for everyday people—that's you and that's me. Together we become *us.* Starting where we are right now, let's walk together, side by side and heart to heart as we commit to make daily simple choices to love God, embrace truth, and enjoy life. Let's offer our moments to God and trust Him to put all our scattered pieces of self together, holy and whole, living well in the daily choices we make one moment at a time.

Girl, it's time to put your holy on!

PART ONE

LOVING GOD
IN EVERY MOMENT

May God himself, the God who makes everything holy and whole, make you holy and whole, put you together—spirit, soul, and body. (1 Thessalonians 5:23 MSG)

CHAPTER 1

MOMENTS TO BELIEVE

> You will have to believe God is who He says He is. You will have
> to believe God can do what He says He will do. You will have to
> adjust your thinking in light of this belief.
>
> —Henry Blackaby, *Experiencing God*

Holiness inhabits the small things, faith for our moments, simple and short. Added together, holy moments change lives and steer destinies in God's direction. But it all comes down to attitudes and choices made . . . one moment at a time.

Just as umbrellas shield us from rain, faith protects us from questions and doubts that flood our souls. When storm clouds gather, an umbrella is only as good as the choosing of it in the moment.

Umbrellas left in the closet or forgotten in the car offer no protection from the deluge. And faith left unused will not shield us from unbelief. Choosing to believe God is a sacred choice, empowering us to "hold up the shield of faith to stop the fiery arrows of the devil" (Ephesians 6:16 NLT).

It's during the storms of life that faith solidifies into more than a concept. The year our family moved from North Carolina to California is the year I thought I was going crazy.

In May of 2000, sunny skies turned dark as storm clouds let loose with a force, whipping and twisting my faith inside out. How do we choose holiness on days when believing God is hard?

WHEN BELIEVING GOD IS HARD

I sat in a stark, utilitarian green office, checking on lab results. "No one called you?" asked a frantic nurse. She explained that my thyroid test (several months old) indicated I have Graves' disease, a hyperthyroid autoimmune disease. Instantly my mind snapped to high alert as I told the nurse, "I'm moving across the country in *three* weeks. We're a military family with three small children. We don't get to choose when or where we move. I *can't* be sick now."

Maybe I hoped the nurse would say something to take the problem away. Something like, "You're right, this isn't a good time for you. Let's reschedule this problem for another time." Our thoughts don't always make sense, do they?

I don't have time to be sick.

It didn't matter. We don't get to schedule challenges at our convenience.

Tested and diagnosed, I was treated with lightning speed. Just take a little pill to slow my thyroid down. *Maybe this won't be too bad*, I thought as packers loaded the moving truck. We drove 3,000 miles with three young kids buckled into our overloaded van. As the miles ticked by, I prayed everything would be OK.

NOW-FAITH IS FOR THIS MOMENT

"Now faith is the assurance of things hoped for, the conviction of things not seen" (Hebrews 11:1 ESV). We need *now-faith* for all of life's moments—the good and the bad. Hope is not wishing, though we often feel like faith is nebulous as cotton candy, wisps of air held together with sugar-coated wishes. *Just have enough faith and you can conjure up whatever you want,* our misconceptions whisper.

Don't we chide ourselves to try harder?

Faith doesn't come by trying harder.

I've made that mistake many times, and it only leads to discouragement. Have you ever been tempted to think you must act better and perform the right spiritual tricks—as if God is only moved to work in a life if the faith is good enough? *Yes, me too!*

That puts it all on us, doesn't it?

Assurance grounds faith in reality—that which has actual existence. It is a steady-minded believing with confidence, courage, and firm trust. There's nothing *maybe-ish* about faith.

Faith is a gift from God, not some secret power we must manufacture on our own. Faith is inseparably tied to the power and holiness of God.

In the Greek, *power* is translated "dynamis," which is God's power for creating life, performing miracles, and righting the crooked soul. This is power we need for all of our *right-now needs*. Every single one.

Choosing faith begins with the holiness of God, not on our ability to harness faith and make it go our way. Faith to believe begins and ends in the rightness of God—His way of doing and being right. "For by grace you have been saved through faith, and that not of yourselves; *it is* the gift of God" (Ephesians 2:8 NKJV, emphasis added).

We make thousands of choices every day. It only takes a moment to respond with *now-faith* and discover more of God. Here's the simple decision of a moment: to believe or not, to trust or not. Holiness is quietly accomplished as we receive the life of Christ in this *now-moment*.

God graciously stirs up more faith when we embrace and live out the faith we currently hold in our hearts. Step by step and choice by choice, we can walk into greater faith and wholeness. "For in it the righteousness of God is revealed from faith for faith; as it is written, 'The righteous shall live by faith'" (Romans 1:17 ESV). In this small three-letter word, *but*, is the choice of the moment.

We can choose the wholeness of believing God, faith for every moment. Or the *buts* can become excuses and questions turning our eyes away from God's power and presence.

I experienced this mentally, physically, and spiritually in a way that tested my faith far beyond the borders of what I thought I could handle. Have you also experienced situations pushing you past your current level of faith?

In the coming months, I learned to rely on God's power to choose faith, one moment at a time. With each choice to believe, God gave me strength to hold on in the moment. There wasn't any other way to get by.

At the end of our cross-country trek, we pulled into military housing in California. We drove slowly down the street, looking for the address of our new home. Tidy, small homes faced the sidewalks where children played. "Is that our house?" piped little voices from the back of the van. More than ready for the end of a long journey, I felt the fresh excitement of new beginnings . . . *until I saw our house.*

Faded yellow paint peeled in spots, and weeds grew two feet tall in cracks of cement. With a hole in the foundation and dead, uncut grass, the house had a dilapidated, musty, uncared-for look. *We're going to live here? Shouldn't this place be condemned?*

This was the moment the imbalance of my hormonal system tipped to a place called *uncontrollable.* Plunging down the steep drop of a thyroid-induced roller coaster, blood pulsed and adrenaline flooded my system; it was months before I felt anything close to calm.

It was months before my hands stopped shaking.

BELIEVING GOD IS A CHOICE, NOT AN EMOTION

Fear stormed in with a take-all vengeance, threatening to wash me away in an unrelenting flood of anxiety. Clouds gathered and my hormonal system cracked open with internal thunder. Dread plagued my days as we got settled, and I tried to care for three young children in an unfamiliar place.

With my body stuck on constant go, sleep became impossible. I spent the dark hours pacing the house, wearing a thin path in the carpet. No matter what I tried, I couldn't turn off my racing thoughts or squelch my feelings of fear.

How do you choose to believe, to stand strong in faith while swirling in overwhelming uncertainties? *I'm going crazy. Will I ever feel normal again?* How do you choose holiness in an iron grip of fear? These are crucial moments to remember that believing in God is a decision, not an emotion.

Many nights I was too jittery to sleep but too weak to stand. While the rest of the family slept, I rocked on my knees pleading, "God, help me!" Heart pounding with my pulse out of control, I longed to unzip my skin and climb right out of myself—be anywhere but stuck in this broken body.

I didn't recognize myself anymore. Who was this frantic, fear-crazed woman taking over my life? Praying like gasping for breath when the water is over your head, I clung to God's promises in Isaiah 43 with the blind strength of a drowning woman gripping a lifeline: "Do not fear, for I have redeemed you; I have called you by name; you are Mine! When you pass through the waters, I will be with you; And through the rivers, they will not overwhelm you" (Isaiah 43:1b-2 AMP). These words helped me hang on, minute by minute.

The soul, the inner life of personality, mind, will, and emotions, is like a deep pool filled with what each of us believe—*really believe*—not just know or agree with.[1] This is the truth we live. Our core beliefs are tucked away in the secrecy of our souls. Some of those beliefs are the truths of God. But others are conclusions and misperceptions based on experiences, thoughts, and emotions impacted by our history. Sometimes truth and false beliefs born of pain and sin lie side by side in the depths of our souls. We have a desperate need for God's healing and restoring work of holiness.

"O Lord, You have searched me and known *me* . . . And are intimately acquainted with all my ways" (Psalm 139:1, 3b, emphasis added). No one knows us better than God. Dallas Willard explained, "You're a soul made by God, made for God, and made to need God, which means you were not made to be self-sufficient."[2] God understands our struggles, and part of holiness is His desire to cleanse us inside and out from the bondage of sin and self.

Given a choice, we would prefer to leap from sinner to sanctified in one quick leap, skipping all the mundane moments and difficult times. But day-by-day, God works to heal our hurts, restore our vision, lift our emotions, guide our steps, and fill our lives with the indwelling Christ. Jesus is the saver, the Savior, of our souls.

Especially in our toughest experiences, holiness is found in each small-but-significant choice to trust God one more time. Inhale another breath and move forward with another shaking step. Never discount small, brave acts of faith that spur you to go on rather than give in. Don't let the hard days keep you from reading God's Word, for truth is lifeblood for our fractured hearts.

Six weeks later and twenty pounds lighter, I was severely sleep-deprived and emotionally strung out with anxiety. Afraid to go out and afraid to stay in, I tried not to give in to fear. I failed again and again, face-planting in the muck of difficulty. God's Spirit strengthened me over and over, reminding me of the passage in Isaiah 43 I had memorized: *When you pass through the waters, I will be with you.*

I was afraid of being afraid.
And through the rivers, they will not overflow you.
I was afraid of nothing specific.
When you walk through the fire, you will not be scorched.
I was afraid of everything.
For I am the LORD your God, the Holy One of Israel, your Savior (vv. 2-3).
Savior. Holy One.
The Lord is my God; He is with me, and He is with you.

Choosing holiness on the hard days comes down to believing God is our Savior who walks with us in all things.

This is true not because it feels true. Fear was the only thing I could feel at this time. Maybe God removed any emotional, warm-fuzzy feeling of His presence to teach me to stand on the truth rather than feelings. To believe God's words were true, I had to stop letting my emotions dictate and define faith.

BELIEVING GOD CONNECTS OUR NEED TO HIS SUPPLY

One foggy morning when taking the kids to school, I pulled up to a stoplight. Staring at the glowing red light, my mind went blank. *Where am I going? Why am I here? I can't remember.* I jerked to consciousness when my son asked, "Mommy, are you going to take us to school?"

That was the day I stopped driving, terrified I would cause an accident.

It's humbling and frightening to realize your sense of sanity is fragile, marked by numbers on a lab report. I just wanted to be well—body, mind, and spirit. I didn't realize I was craving holiness.

What does holiness have to do with wellness? The answer is a lot, actually. Early roots of the English word *holy* mean "whole, uninjured, healthy, complete, and happy."

Daily I prayed for healing, for the problem to go away, only to struggle with another sleepless night filled with fear.

I wanted relief, but God wanted growth.

In this strange and scary time, God supplied my needs through His Word and through the kindness of people who helped in practical ways. My active-duty husband was assigned to a school, so he was home every night, a God-gift for a military family. Before we even moved in, the first friend I made was Jennifer, a pharmacist. She answered endless medical questions and helped me navigate the complexity of my symptoms. Always cheerful, she invited us to explore our new community, getting me out of the house.

Living on a military base meant I was surrounded by women who knew the challenges of moving. My neighbor Liz could look at me and know when I needed help. She would say, "Bring the girls over so you can try to take a nap." After a rest, we'd drink coffee and visit. Her calm spirit and strong faith were also God-gifts. Recognizing the practical ways God helped and provided gave me hope.

During these anxiety-ridden days and nights, I read Bible verses again and again. I said them softly, prayed them in the dark, and even yelled them at times: "Don't fret or worry. Instead of worrying, pray. Let petitions and praises shape your worries into prayers, letting God know your concerns. Before you know it, a sense of God's wholeness, everything coming together for good, will come and settle you down. It's wonderful what happens when Christ displaces worry at the center of your life" (Philippians 4:6-7 MSG).

God heard from me plenty—as in constantly—as I took this passage to heart with *now-faith*. Worries became prayers, transforming emotions into choices to believe. And I waited long and hard for a sense of God's wholeness to settle my soul.

Day after day, I wrote notes to God in my journal, pouring out my heart with a mix of prayers and complaints. I copied verses in my book, grasping each promise of strength as God brought them to my attention.

- I'm still feeling terrible, not sleeping. Praying for deliverance. Lord, give me the ability to choose faith today. Help me to trust You. —10/15/2000
- It's so hard to take care of the children. Will You help me do all the things I need to do? I'm so tired of being anxious and weak. I'm barely hanging on today, Lord. —11/5/2000
- I can do all things in Him who strengthens me—You're going to have to bring the strength, for I don't have any. Today, I can hardly walk across the street. —11/20/2000

- Who am I? Where did the best parts of me go? I hate the person I'm becoming. Is this really part of your plan? —12/5/2000
- I believe You are the God who makes me holy and whole, but I'm falling apart in broken pieces. I'm leaving a trail of worry and fear everywhere I go. PLEASE put me together—spirit, soul, and body! (1 Thessalonians 5:23a *rephrased*). —12/15/2000

CHOOSING HOLY IN THE HARD

As the California fall days melted into the fog of my mental state, I had numerous medical appointments. Before finding a specialist, I saw a physician's assistant. "I have Graves' disease, and I haven't slept in a month," I said, desperate for something to help me sleep. This young man glossed over the one-month-no-sleep part, asking, "Have you tried hot milk?" I'm not going into details, but for me, this was definitely a most unholy moment. I considered scratching his eyes out but restrained myself . . . barely.

God reminded me of the story of Abraham, the one who believed God's promise of a child even though he was impossibly old. A child from Sarah's old and shriveled womb? *Really?* "Yet, with respect to the promise of God, he did not waver in unbelief but grew strong in faith, giving glory to God, and being fully assured that what God had promised, He was able also to perform. Therefore it was also credited to him as righteousness" (Romans 4:20-22).

Faith is conviction of truth, belief in God, including the idea of trust and holy fervor born of faith.

Faith walks hand in hand with holiness.

- Growing strong in this case means to be strengthened or given strength. God was the source of this strength for Abraham's choice to believe.

- God viewed Abraham's faith as righteousness—a word closely related to *holiness,* meaning "integrity, virtue, purity of life, and rightness."
- Receiving strength to believe is a holy moment and a gift from God.

That Christmas, I experienced God's strength in a miraculous way. My mother flew out to join us for the holiday. After the long flight from Tennessee, she was exhausted. This was strange for a woman with more energy than three of me. Too tired to eat dinner, she went to bed, as I grew more and more concerned. In my anxious state, I could feel the first wave of fear roll through my system. "No, not now, Lord! I can't give in to fear. I need Your strength and a calm heart," I prayed. That night, my mom had a stroke brought on by the air travel. Where do you find holiness in the middle of a stroke?

- Turning to God in prayer is choosing holy in the hard.
- Choosing to believe God is good is choosing holy in the hard.
- Recognizing God's provision in our need is *experiencing* holy in the hard.

One holy choice: Not every moment is good, but believe God is good in every moment.

Waiting for the EMTs to arrive, my pulse slowed to a steady calm I hadn't known in months. In the middle of my ordinary, broken life, I experienced wholeness through God's gift of strength. By all counts, this emergency should have sent me over the edge.

My hands stopped shaking.

My mind was clear.

My heart settled with a long-forgotten peace.

I believe Jesus spoke to the storm in my mind and body, with a divine command, "Peace, be still." Right at the time I needed it most. No wavering. No shaking. All grace.

Three days later, Mom was released from the hospital with minor issues. Her left hand was clumsy-slow and one foot dragged heavily, but she was improving. She came home on Christmas Eve, spunky and determined to attend church for the candlelight service. With a grateful heart beating slowly and steadily, I experienced a Christmas miracle—both for Mom and for myself.

As the anxiety lifted and sleep returned, God gave me strength to help my mom. A few weeks later, doctors used radiation to destroy my thyroid, continuing my physical process of healing. This challenging year ended with a Christmas so special that tears flow at the memory as I write. The warm glow of candles and the presence of God filled the church as we raised our voices singing with pure, clear tones.

> Silent night, Holy night
> All is calm, all is bright
> Round yon virgin, Mother and child
> Holy infant so tender and mild
> *Sleep in heavenly peace.*

SIMPLE WAYS TO BELIEVE GOD

- Ask God for the faith you need for this moment—*use your umbrella.*
- This is your moment to believe. Trust God with your *right-now need.*
- Don't let emotions define your faith.
- Watch for ways God provides.
- Write, pray, and memorize specific truths to strengthen your faith.
- Accept help and encouragement from friends. Don't isolate yourself.
- Believe God has given the faith you ask for and take a step forward.

YOUR MOMENT TO BELIEVE

How about you? What need is before you? Are you buffeted by emotions, making faith hard to hold? Identify your *right-now need* for faith. Is it fear or frustration? A diagnosis or a decision? Faith is the power anchoring hope to our souls with the grit of determination to believe God and to discover holiness in the hard. Rest in this moment and stand under the power of one sacred choice to trust God, to hang onto hope *right here, right now.*

Holding on is the strength of holiness working in the moment.

Now-faith is for the anxious and rainy moments—the drizzles, the showers, and even the downpours threatening to wash you way. Open your umbrella and choose holiness that is solid ground when dreams grow soggy at your feet.

Don't wait for the rain to stop. In daily life, umbrellas are for the rain, but faith is for the spiritual storms. In the middle of my ordinary, broken life, I experienced wholeness through God's gift of strength.

SIMPLE REMINDERS TO BELIEVE

- Choose *now-faith* for this moment.
- Faith doesn't come by trying harder.
- A gift from God, faith isn't some secret power you must manufacture.
- Faith is inseparably tied to the power and holiness of God.
- Believing God is a decision, not an emotion.
- Don't let the hard days keep you from reading God's Word.
- Believing God connects your need to His supply.
- Not every moment is good, but believe God is good in every moment.

CHAPTER 2

MOMENTS TO CHOOSE

Holiness is not simply what God gives me, but what God has
given me that is being exhibited in my life.

—Oswald Chambers, *My Utmost for His Highest*

Days are made of hours; hours are made of minutes; minutes are made of
seconds. Change the moment and transform the hours filling our days. Split-
second decisions can change our attitudes when we trust God to transform
the heart. Grace to live well in little choices is the blessing we crave.

We long to fold our hearts around joy each day. Desires, questions, and
aspirations spin willy-nilly in our heads. Time slips like sand through our fingers. How do we make the best use of the time given, each day wrapped in the
gift of twenty-four hours?

To tell you the truth, too much of my mental and physical time is spent
trying to get it all together in some perfectly performing package of worthi-
ness. What's possible when we stop trying to make ourselves better and simply trust God to guide, help, and provide in each moment as it comes? What's
released when we trust God's truth in the small moments of our days?

My thoughts rest on one word: *holiness.* Though this word sometimes
suggests stale religion bound tightly with pious *dos* and *don'ts*, holiness is a
refreshingly simple concept. You won't find it sitting on a shelf of musty, old
books no one wants to read. When we look, we discover the sacred in our
everyday moments, not moments far off, hidden in prayers of monks or waiting for the next spiritual mountaintop experience.

I remember insecure days as a teenager when I was concerned about my place in the ranked society of *who's in* and *who's out*. One day I overheard a snide comment, "Oh, don't invite her; she's a holy roller." I shrank back, hurt and feeling left out.

No longer a teenager, I still don't want to be known by a label. Holiness to the world can be a put-down, and yet for so long I saw it as a lofty goal, hovering somewhere beyond my reach. Now I see it differently: Holiness has a practical side—one that is for relying on Christ in my everyday moments.

On days when consecration feels more like a cold code of conduct or a test to pass, consider the profound love expressed in these words: "Blessed be the God and Father of our Lord Jesus Christ, who has blessed us with every spiritual blessing in the heavenly places in Christ, just as He chose us in Him before the foundation of the world, that we would be holy and blameless before Him" (Ephesians 1:3-4).

One of our *spiritual blessings*, holiness doesn't depend on our ability to be perfect, although we often try.

Holiness begins with a choice, a choice God made when He chose you.

Long before you were born, nestled in the beginning of everything, God chose you, and He chose me. When we commit to believe Christ is our Savior, we are made holy and blameless. God "settled on us as the focus of his love, to be made whole and holy by his love" (Ephesians 1:4 MSG). Sacred, pure, and devoted, holiness begins with God, who chooses to work in our lives, cleansing our hearts so we can love Him with heart, soul, and mind.

Holy in the moment can be as simple as our thoughts, words, and actions as we commit to love God, embrace truth, and enjoy life. Making intentional choices to trust God is where holiness happens right in the middle of an ordinary day.

A day just like today.

Sunlight streams through the window as autumn leaves paint the light with a warm glow. I would enjoy the beauty of the day, but the flecks of dust floating in the air distract me, landing in a thick layer on the table. I should stop and clean the table, but it's littered with an odd assortment of items I've been too busy to put away. Newspapers to discard, a box to mail, bills to pay, and my unread Bible—*when did my Bible begin gathering dust?*

How did I get so busy that clearing the table of collected debris of hectic days is more than I can keep up with? The table isn't the only problem. The house is a mess, and my life is getting that way as well. I can't think straight when clutter crowds out clarity, but I don't have time to fix it now.

The busier life gets, the more disrupted my internal routines become. Papers multiply into piles, missed workouts turn into pounds, neglected friends become acquaintances, and stress pulses like blood through bulging veins.

My unsettled soul is out of sync with what is true. *Again.*

Too weary to stop, I feel my life pulling apart, fraying at the seams. I long for the vitality of fresh faith to wash me clean from sin and self-centeredness. Insecurities whisper loudly and selfish desires overtake good intentions. I indulge in negative thought as if it were hot fudge on ice cream, yet the taste is bitter to my heart.

Frustration fights with peace until I finally turn.

Lay it down.

Let it go.

Repentant, I ignore the dust, opening my Bible with an apology on my lips instead of a prayer. God's encouragement reminds me of what I have known but forgotten. He speaks kindly to my self-condemning thoughts.

I will wash away false pressures and tempting distractions. Your task is to come. Surrender yourself as a living and holy sacrifice. Put your heart into My hand and learn to rest in the grace-filled truth that renewing the soul out of sync is My specialty.

HOLINESS IS A SECRET TO A LIFE WELL LIVED

Is holiness a distant concept to you? Are you becoming the whole person God created you to be? Did you realize, in Christ, you *are* holy? You have the righteousness of Christ that is yours once you believe Jesus is your Savior (2 Corinthians 5:21). You may not always feel pure and righteous, but God is in the process of transforming your mind, will, and emotions—your soul—to align with the new identity you received at your spiritual birth.

So what's the problem? Why don't we feel or recognize the truth that we are righteous on a daily basis? Just yesterday, a friend commented, "I know the fact that I am holy, but I don't feel holy. I struggle to think of myself as holy." We all wrestle with sin and selfish desires conflicting with godly living. No one is exempt from the process of growing in holiness. Galatians 5:16 (NASB) tells us to "walk by the Spirit, and you will not carry out the desire of the flesh."

A biblical word meaning human nature apart from God, our flesh is prone to sin and is independent from God. *Flesh* is also described as "the old ways or patterns by which you have attempted to get all your needs supplied instead of seeking Christ first and trusting Him to meet your needs."[1] For me, this simple question is helpful: Am I choosing flesh or spirit in this situation? As believers, we now have choices available, grounded in trusting God—choices that make a difference.

Purity shines as we learn to think, feel, and love from the resource of Christ rather than our self-effort. Wholehearted living comes through trusting God. This may sound like a lot of spiritual *holier-than-thou* kind of talk, but it is profoundly practical. Sacred simplicity is a secret to a life well lived when we make the most of all our moments for God to change our lives one spiritual choice at a time.

We streamline our complicated, busy lives when we trust God, rely on His wisdom, and live from His resources each day. Consider this verse: "May God himself, the God who makes everything holy and whole, make you holy and whole, put you together—spirit, soul, and body—and keep you fit for the coming of our Master, Jesus Christ. The One who called you is completely dependable. If he said it, he'll do it" (1 Thessalonians 5:23-24 MSG). We experience grace as God begins to put our fragmented pieces together, and we respond through the daily choices we make. The Bible sometimes refers to the process of God making us holy as *sanctification*, transforming our hearts and lives by the renewing of our souls.

"God hasn't invited us into a disorderly, unkempt life but into something holy and beautiful—as beautiful on the inside as the outside" (1 Thessalonians 4:7 MSG). The idea that God restores internal order, spiritual wholeness, and inner beauty is a whole new spin on the concept of holiness for me. Maybe for you too.

HOW PRACTICAL IS HOLINESS?

Holiness is good for nothing if it is simply a label. Yet when we rely on Christ and choose God's ways *right here, right now* in this minute, God will change our lives one day at a time.

Sacred choices, in spite of what they may look like, enable us to live full of God and full with God. Holiness comes in all shapes, sizes, and situations, and it isn't just for churchy activities and our Sunday best. In the middle of mess and confusion, we can choose to depend on God's strength. I'm talking about a when-the-kids-are-screaming holiness. The I'm-in-the-middle-of-a-fight holiness. The I'm-grumpy-and-you're-bugging-me holiness. Sanctity doesn't come from situations but from the presence of Christ in us and the faith choices we make.

Sacred simplicity is ours when we live life wholly, dedicated with purpose and meaning. This is something I long for in a complicated and chaotic world where I often feel insignificant and small.

Holiness comes when we make room for God in our busy lives, offering our hearts just as they are, not as we wish they were.

"Therefore I urge you, brethren, by the mercies of God, to present your bodies a living and holy sacrifice, acceptable to God, *which is* your spiritual service of worship" (Romans 12:1, emphasis added).

What is this living and holy sacrifice God wants us to make with our bodies, our physical lives? This Greek verb for the word *living* (*zao*) has to do with enjoying real life that comes from Christ. It's energetic, fresh, and strong, bringing the power of God into the way we live and act. *The Message* puts it this way: "God helping you: Take your everyday, ordinary life—your sleeping, eating, going-to-work, and walking-around life—and place it before God as an offering" (Romans 12:1 MSG).

Isn't it a relief to recognize we don't have to *make ourselves* faultless and acceptable to God? Rather than requiring our perfection, God simply asks us to offer ourselves, to place our lives in His hands. We do the offering, the surrendering, to let God take care of the making. We offer our time, effort, gifts, skills, and obedience, but we trust God for the results. Depending on God to work through our efforts brings God into the present in our awareness. On our part, holiness also begins with a choice—the choice to offer our everyday moments to God.

Wrapped tightly in our flesh is a frenetic tendency to make life complicated. My soul is hardwired with an intense desire for significance, and I think yours is too. Feeling less, we take on more, and *try harder, be better, do more* is the rant of souls that have swallowed the compelling lies of this chaotic, bent world. The myth that we can *do it all, have it all,* and *be it all* drives us to lose focus with too many *yeses* and too many *shoulds*. And we *yes* and *yes* ourselves into a worn-out, scattered frenzy. *Hold up, Holy Girl, these are choices we make when we lose sight of offering ourselves to God, seeking His best.*

DISCOVER THE SIMPLICITY
OF OFFERING

As I write these words, I glance over at my to-do list scrawled on bits of paper, a small city of yellow notes stuck to my desk. Reminders of commitments made, every single one is something I said "yes" to. *Have I tried to do too much? How will I do it all?* And all too soon it will be time to make dinner.

I write goals with bold letters of good intention. Finishing my to-do list is one of those goals. Too often faith becomes an exercise in good behavior and self-improvement—trying to make myself perfect and pleasing to God. Confusing holiness with productivity and performance, I scurry through the day leaving a trail of the undone that calls out condemnations and validates my fears that I'm not enough. Too often our harried busyness erodes our relationship with God and *later* becomes our spiritual growth plan.

Sound familiar?

I shift in my chair and take a long, slow breath. I can't agree to one more request, or the whole house of cards is going to come tumbling down. With a quick prayer, I focus on one thing at a time, trusting God will enable me to complete all He desires me to finish. I want to stay alert, offering my heart, time, and attention to what God desires to do in this small pocket of time.

Looking at my crazy, mixed-up list, the tension in my neck relaxes.

My perspective shifts from the pressure of doing to the simplicity of offering. Somehow, this becomes a practical act of reverence, right here in the midst of a thousand things to do today.

How about you? What could happen if you pull back the throttle that keeps you running on continual overdrive, offering God your heart and your trust one day at a time? Let's give God our best as we trust Him to put us together, holy and whole, in this moment. *Holy Girl, this is the choice that makes all the difference.*

SIMPLE REMINDERS FOR EVERY MOMENT

- Holiness is a gift from God, not a cold code of conduct.
- God has set you apart for the purpose of being made whole or complete.
- Holiness begins with the choice God made when He chose you.
- Practice reverence by relying on Christ in the moment.
- Shift your perspective from the pressure of doing to the simplicity of offering.
- Holy moments will change your life from the inside out.
- Make deliberate choices to love God, embrace truth, and enjoy life.

CHAPTER 3

MOMENTS TO LOVE GOD

Our only business is to love and delight ourselves in God.

—Brother Lawrence, *Practicing the Presence of God*

Holiness doesn't have an age limit, and loving God doesn't require special qualifications.

I still remember the smell of the chunky crayon as I drew a big red heart on construction paper. I am in second grade, and Mrs. Pierce is my Sunday school teacher. She is nice, laughs often, and wears pointy blue glasses. Ruth Ann sits next to me, and her heart looks better than mine, neat with all the crayon strokes going the same direction.

My coloring is wild and scribbly with an energy that won't stay in the lines.

"Do you know why we are drawing hearts today?" asks Mrs. Pierce. With the ease of a woman who loves children, she tells us the greatest thing we can do is to love God. She reads the big-print Bible on her lap: "The Lord our God is one Lord; and you shall love the Lord your God with all your heart, and with all your soul, and with all your mind, and with all your strength" (Mark 12:29-30).

Pressing the crayon harder into the paper, I color faster as I listen. Even at seven years old, I know there is something special about these words. As a child, I had no concept of holiness, but "love God with all your heart" is etched into my mind with the memory of big red hearts drawn in second-grade Sunday school days.

Don't make things too complicated.

Sometimes we get all theological and lofty about spiritual topics. In our efforts to understand, we complicate simple truths, making them seem difficult.

Loving God with all your heart is a holy thing. It is what we're created for, and when we love God we fulfill our purpose. Isn't this what we're searching for? Godly lives are built on a foundation of loving God.

SIMPLE WAYS TO LOVE GOD WITH THE HEART OF A CHILD

I'm still learning how to give God my whole heart with simple faith. Loving God is the journey of a lifetime, and there is always more to discover. It's a never-ending story if we keep seeking to worship Him.

- Take delight in small pleasures.
- Reach for God like a child lifts arms to be held.
- Twirl in the sunlight just for the joy of being alive.
- Imagine resting your head on God's shoulder.
- Get excited because Daddy's home.
- Greet each day with the fresh joy of a child.

What ways can you love God like a child today? How can you make intentional choices to express your adoration for God this week?

LOVE GOD WITH THE HEART OF A MOTHER

Years later, I am no longer a child, and my perspective shifts dramatically the day I become a mother.

I look down at a tiny hand, fingers curled around my index finger with surprising strength. Tears in my eyes, I am stunned by the sheer miracle of holding this long-awaited baby in my arms for the very first time. This moment is profound and sacred.

Nothing could have prepared me for the tearing pain of the delivery or the awe of experiencing the wonder of new life. He is just minutes old, and his first frantic cries have settled. Maternal love wells up swift and strong with a weight that is a glimmer of the glory of God.

In the days to come, my husband and I admire his itty-bitty toes and the wide-eyed alert expression in his eyes. We love him fiercely. He is our son. This love has nothing to do with abilities, personality, or looks. We don't have to grow into this feeling or warm up to it in any way. We cherish him simply because he is *our* son.

I pat his back as he sleeps on my shoulder, his cheek warm against my neck. I begin to understand a deeper layer of the Father-heart of God. Though I have known since I was seven that God is my Father, now I understand in a new way that I am loved simply because I am His child. I shake my head as I realize deep down how many times I've labored to believe this simple truth:

God loves me because I am His child. It *really* is that simple.

Looks, personality, abilities, performance, or behavior do not earn God's affection any more than I would wait to love until my son is old enough to help with the chores or even express His love for me.

How do I care for You more than this baby in my arms, Lord? I know I'm supposed to love God above all else, but right now . . . I'm not sure how. How do I love a God I cannot see more than this helpless infant sleeping in my arms?

The fact I'm asking the question hints at the answer.

Laying my son beside me, I write the question in my journal, ready to wrestle with it. Words scratching across the page, God brings forth a new insight through the words I write.

Let your love for your child teach you a deeper love for Me. Enjoy the gift. Learn from the gift, but always let the gift turn your heart to the Giver. Experience your love for others in the context of My love for you.

So simple.

Why do we obscure this gift we are created to give? Knowing the unconditional love I have for my child helps me to understand a little more of God's love.

In the quiet of the night, my son sleeps peacefully, and time slows as the Spirit shows me another way of loving God. This baby rests with no thought or concern in the safety of my care. Loving God is to rest peacefully in the circle of His everlasting arms, just as my child sleeps, belly full and safe from harm. "Return to your rest, O my soul, for the LORD has dealt bountifully with you" (Psalm 116:7).

In this moment, I breathe deeply and relax, reveling in the truth that my life is in His watchful care. "We know it so well, we've embraced it heart and soul, this love that comes from God" (1 John 4:16 MSG).

What ways has God drawn you into a deeper love for Him through the joy of loving others?

Let your love for family draw you deeper into a grateful love for God.

Reflect on how loving others can enable you to worship Him more deeply. How can you cherish God right now?

LOVING GOD WHEN YOU FEEL UNLOVABLE

She's a woman with a past ruined with hard living and bad choices. She can't remember the last time she could walk down the street and not see condemning stares or feel the heat of shame creeping up her neck. When was the last time life was good and hope seemed real?

Hanging her head, she tries to slip by unseen. Women stand outside houses chattering about their children as the hot sun beats down. She feels even more alone. She walks faster as the women notice her. She'd run if she could, just to avoid the pain of facing what she's become. She's notorious, a wicked sinner—probably the worst in town. Fingers point as pleasant talk turns ugly with snide comments. Over the sound of the breeze, she can hear the condemning gossip recounting her latest sins.

They're not saying anything worse than what she says to herself.

How can she find forgiveness to start fresh when she can't even forgive herself?

How can she love God when she feels unlovable down to the core of every poor choice she has ever made? Why would a righteous God want her devotion?

If "hopeless" were an ocean, she'd be drowning.

The conversation turns as someone asks, "Did you hear Simon invited the Rabbi—that Jesus—to dine at his house today?" Her heart stops for a breath as a tiny spark of hope flickers. Could He? Would He? Forgive *her*?

Sometime later, Jesus reclines at a table having dinner with Simon, a respected religious leader.

Bold with desperation, this woman acts with courage born of one last hope to turn a wreck of a life around. She is nameless, known only by a label: sinner. Some might say she is grasping for the wind by daring to enter Simon's house. Uninvited, she weeps loud and hard, as broken-hearted women mourn their dead. The pain and bitterness of knowing exactly what she is can no longer be contained in the presence of the One who heals the sick and forgives the sinner.

Tears won't stop as she begins to wash His feet. Kissing His feet, she doesn't dare to look up. With shaking hands, she wipes His feet with her hair. She pours out the only thing of value she has left, a small vial of perfume. It is the last bit of the life she dreamed of long ago.

PRIDE HINDERS LOVE FOR GOD

"Now when the Pharisee who had invited Him saw this, he said to himself, 'If this man were a prophet He would know who and what sort of person this woman is who is touching Him, that she is a sinner'" (Luke 7:39).

The weeping sinner stands stark against the judgmental pride of the religious man. Simon, confident in his position as a Jewish leader, looks on with disdain that follows self-importance. Worlds apart, Simon has done all the right things while this woman has thrown her life away.

Past and position couldn't be further apart between Simon and the woman, but Jesus reveals the greatest difference is the condition of their hearts.

Criticism comes easily.

Oh, so easily.

Simon cannot see this woman as a humble sinner, desperate for forgiveness and undone with devotion for Christ. With distorted vision, Simon sees himself as the one in the right. After all, he is in the business of loving God, or so it would seem.

Telling a simple story, Jesus reveals Simon's faults, uncovering the cracks in the façade of his self-righteousness: "'A moneylender had two debtors: one owed five hundred denarii, and the other fifty. When they were unable to repay, he graciously forgave them both. So which of them will love him more?' Simon answered and said, 'I suppose the one whom he forgave more.' And He said to him, 'You have judged correctly'" (Luke 7:41-43).

The woman knows her sins and seeks forgiveness. Simon, confident in his own righteousness, has nothing but disapproval for both Christ and the woman.

In this moment, the tables have turned, and Simon is the sinner.

"Do you see this woman? I entered your house; you gave Me no water for My feet, but she has wet My feet with her tears and wiped them with her hair. You gave Me no kiss; but she, *since the time I came in, has not ceased* to kiss My feet. You did not anoint My head with oil, but she anointed My feet with perfume. For this reason I say to you, her sins, which are many, have been forgiven, for she loved much; but he who is forgiven little, loves little." Then He said to her, "Your sins have been forgiven." (Luke 7:44-48, emphasis added)

Rather than condemning the sinner, Jesus points out the many ways Simon lacks common courtesy and the ways the woman shows devotion.

- Simon neglected to welcome his guest with a kiss, a glaring oversight compared to the woman's emotional act of devotion.
- The woman washes His feet with the intimacy of raw emotion. Reverence and gratitude turn a servant's chore into an act of worship and a sinner's repentance into a moment for mercy. From mundane to sanctified is a short step when motivated by love for God.
- She has no concern about what the others think of her actions. All she can see is an opportunity to show love and gratitude at the mere chance of forgiveness.
- This woman knows her sins, longs to be forgiven, and seeks Christ deeply.

OVERCOME BARRIERS TO LOVING GOD

How about you? Have obstacles or distractions hindered your intentional choices to love God? Has feeling unworthy or unforgivable distanced you from God? Subtle and often invisible to others, these are a few barriers to loving God in this passage.

1. Many invite Christ in but neglect to welcome and honor Him with worship. *"You did not even . . ."* No one wants to hear Jesus say these words, but we often overlook the minimal expressions of worship and devotion. Busy schedules and technology-overload consume our time and attention. Take time to welcome Christ as you begin your day. Show adoration for God by expressing humble gratitude for His love and forgiveness. Determine to be aware of God in the various activities of your day.

2. Don't be the Pharisee, prideful and self-righteous, confident you know best. How easy it is to criticize others rather than to consider the stale conditions of our own hearts. The more honestly we see ourselves, the more godly sorrows and contrite hearts enable us to love Jesus, the One who forgives without reservation. Love God with honest humility and confession of sin.

3. Reject the lie that you can't be forgiven. Perhaps you are the woman who feels there is no hope for real forgiveness and change. You've gone too far for too long, and you're sinking in a sea of hopelessness. Maybe you've done things you never thought you'd do and you can't forgive yourself. *"How can God possibly forgive me?"* is the thought torturing your soul.

You want to love God, but you fear you aren't worthy of His esteem. Are you ready for a fresh start? It's time for holy confidence as you hold on to this truth: You are forgiven. "If we confess our sins, He is faithful and righteous to forgive us our sins and to cleanse us from all unrighteousness" (1 John 1:9).

MAKE A SIMPLE CHOICE TO POUR YOUR HEART OUT TO GOD

"Trust in Him at all times, O people; Pour out your heart before Him; God is a refuge for us" (Psalm 62:8).

Be inspired by the boldness of this nameless woman. Prayerfully put yourself in her place. Pour out your heart to Christ and believe you will be forgiven just like this brave, broken woman weeping at the feet of Jesus. Imagine filling a bucket with all the sins and situations making you feel unloved or unworthy of forgiveness. If you've never accepted Christ as your Savior, make this your day to invite Him into your life. Unwrap the gift of holiness in your life when you choose salvation.

Choose to believe. Don't let this moment slip by. If you're a hands-on person, write your hurts, fears, and sinful choices on paper and actually put them in a bucket of water to represent your tears. Prayerfully dump your bucket and your heart before your God who loves you *no matter what.*

As you pour out your troubles, believe Jesus has forgiven your sins. Today, hold fast to faith and let go of condemnation. Ask for forgiveness and let gratitude deepen your love for God. "For He rescued us from the domain of darkness, and transferred us to the kingdom of His beloved Son, in whom we have redemption, the forgiveness of sins" (Colossians 1:13).

Forgiveness is a foundation for growth and healing. This is our reverent offering, releasing our brokenness into the loving hands of God who makes us holy and whole. Let Jesus set right your soul and listen to Him whisper in your ear, "Your sins have been forgiven. . . . Your faith has saved you; go in peace" (Luke 7: 48, 50).

Repeat this truth every time doubt tempts you to hang onto the weight of guilt or condemnation: *I am completely forgiven, and I am holy.*

Sin does not disqualify you from God's love. Receive forgiveness and open the floodgate of your grateful heart.

LOVING GOD IS OUR BEST KIND OF HOLY

"To love the LORD your God with all your heart and with all your soul, so that you may live. . . . For this commandment which I command you today is not too difficult for you, nor is it out of reach" (Deuteronomy 30:6b, 11).

With purpose and authority, Moses gives a final charge to a new generation of Israelites. Ready to enter the Promised Land, the dream of a lifetime, these people are ready to brave the unknown. They grew up in the shadow of their parents' doubt and false courage that fled in the face of giants. They've spent their youth wandering dusty desert trails, waiting for this day.

This is their time.

Now is their moment to enter fully into the promise of God.

They fiercely need to hear *one more time* the simple truth of what is most important—the one thing marking the difference between life or death, victory or defeat, blessing or curse.

Loving God with heart and soul is choosing life—the life God designed for us to live. The life that enters the promise and overcomes the enemy.

Worshiping God is for all our moments, but we often divide our devotion to God. Compartmentalizing life like slices of pie, we offer Him one slice and keep the rest for ourselves.

What does this tendency look like in the comings and goings of a day? For me, it looks a lot like yesterday. I volunteer to watch children so young moms can attend a Bible study. After a day's work, however, the last thing I wanted to do yesterday was spend the evening wiping noses and listening to babies cry in the church nursery. Feeling tired, I served out of obligation. Love motivated by obligation isn't truly love. The words, *"I love God with all my heart. . ."* roll off my tongue easily, but my thoughts are consumed with a thousand other things.

Holy in the moment, I want love for my God to motivate all I do—work, serve, rest, and play. Delighting in God is choosing the wonderful life we were created to live. What else is there?

No tricks, no holding back, and no insincerity—this is what God asks of us. *Keep it real. Keep it holy.*

SIMPLE WAYS TO LOVE GOD IN THE MOMENT

- What are you feeling today, the emotions that shift and swing? *Trust God in the midst of those emotions . . . all of them.*

- What do you need today, the big and needy as well as the small and mundane? *Rely on God and trust Him with your needs. Every single one.*
- What are you delighting in today; what little blessings are bringing a smile to your face? *Honor God through your joy and celebrate His goodness.*
- What demands your strength today, the tasks and responsibilities piling at your feet? *Worship God as you work.*
- What are you thinking? *Open your mind and offer your thoughts with love and honesty.*

Love God with the heart of a child, the wonder of a mother, and the gratitude of a sinner.

Your days matter, and each one is a fresh opportunity to love God in the midst of a busy life. As we learn to love God with our lives, He will break through barriers of distraction, insincerity, and sin because we have invited Him in with love. One faithful way to navigate today: remember to love God with your whole life. What could happen when you make the commitment to worship God in the midst of it all?

Loving God is our greatest command, our significant purpose, and our deepest need. Worship consecrates the day, so *set this moment apart*—make it holy by bringing your heart to God. His arms are open wide for you.

Oh yes, loving God with your life is the best kind of holy.

SIMPLE REMINDERS FOR LOVING GOD

- Choose to love God with the simple heart of a child.
- Let your love for family draw you deeper into a grateful love for God.
- Come to God even when you feel unlovable.

- Don't play the Pharisee—prideful, self-righteous, and sure you know best.
- Reject the lie that you can't be forgiven.
- Delighting in God is choosing the wonderful life you were created to live.
- Loving God is your greatest command, significant purpose, and deepest need.
- Loving God is your best kind of holy.

CHAPTER 4

MOMENTS TO ABIDE

What gives our moments meaning is not the moments
themselves but the presence of Christ with us in the midst of
them.

—Emily P. Freeman, *Simply Tuesday*

The day draws to a close. It's the magic hour when the sun casts a golden glow,
tilting shadows, and making all seem right with the world. Walking down
a path to the beach, the older children run ahead, but my youngest daughter reaches out to hold my hand. "Mommy, I like walking with you. Will we
always walk together like this?" she asks with the innocent wisdom of a four-
year-old. I answer, "There's nothing I'd like better."

Abiding in Christ is like this walk with my little girl. Our relationship connects us, and it is a sweet joy to hold her small hand, to steady her steps when
she trips, to answer her questions, and to listen to her excitement.

When Jesus talked about abiding, He explained, "I am the vine, you are
the branches; he who abides in Me and I in him, he bears much fruit, for apart
from Me you can do nothing" (John 15:5). The relationship between the vine
and the branches is clear. In reality, branches don't need a three-step formula
or a five-day plan to bear fruit. The industrious part of me that always wants
a plan begins to relax a bit. Simply staying connected enables the branch to
receive what it needs to thrive.

Abiding is a natural connection with God. In the book, *Soul Keeping*,
John Ortberg explains the importance of seeing all our moments "under the

care and connection of God. To focus on myself apart from God means losing awareness of what matters most."[1]

Holding hands on a walk and a fruit-bearing branch on the vine—thinking about these concrete images gives a fresh glimpse of the grace-gift of abiding. Smiling inside and out, I remember God's companionship in the midst of a playful afternoon with my children. Today abiding is simple *and* fun. *Hmm . . . this isn't so hard after all.*

ABIDING BEGINS WITH GOD'S INVITATION

Because our bodies lose water through breathing, sweating, digesting—daily living at the most basic level—we need to continually drink water. What's true of our bodies is also true of our souls.

On a hot, dusty day long ago, a woman draws water from the town well. Right in the middle of her daily routine—her work and her avoiding, her need and her issues—Jesus comes to her. A divine appointment in the midst of everyday life. He starts a conversation with this woman who's made far too many mistakes trying to fill her heart with love in the arms of too many men.

Asking for a drink of water, Jesus tells her, "Whoever drinks of the water that I will give him shall never thirst; but the water that I will give him will become in him a well of water springing up to eternal life" (John 4:13-14).

We know her only as the nameless woman at the well. Could it be she is in some way any woman? Or even every woman? For haven't we all tried to quench our thirst with water we've drawn ourselves and fill our hearts with efforts of our own making? Haven't we all made our mistakes, substituting the love of others for the love of God? These are the things that keep us from abiding.

I may not know her name, but I know this woman in my heart. I recognize glimpses of her when I look in the mirror. I hear her in the depths of my desire to find acceptance and approval from others. Like her, I've looked for fulfillment in too many things other than Christ: marriage, parenting, work, and appearance to name a few. Yes, I know this woman in a personal way. You probably do too.

To come and never thirst again is the divine invitation of an audaciously generous God. Jesus is the One who seeks out sinners and finds us even at the wells where we seek life and meaning from insufficient sources. A vital part of abiding is seeing our needs and choosing to respond as Christ speaks life to the parched places of our soul.

To the pure and the unholy, the saints and the sinners, the invitation is the same. Without reprimands, rules, or rituals, Jesus invites with three simple words we can choose in every moment: come and drink.

"He who believes in Me [who adheres to, trusts in, and relies on Me], as the Scripture has said, 'From his innermost being will flow *continually* rivers of living water'" (John 7:38 AMP, emphasis added). This surplus is the promise, the natural outcome of Jesus' invitation to abide. As we receive, the Holy Spirit wells up and overflows as God releases Himself.

More than we need.

More than enough.

More than we can contain.

Choose holy in the moment, and live in the overflow.

Rather than plans, procedures, or programs, simply receive. When A. B. Simpson struggled to grow in holiness, he wrote, "I had to learn to take from Himself my spiritual life every second, to breathe Himself in as I breathed, and breathe myself out. So, moment by moment for the spirit, and moment by moment for the body, we must receive."[2]

God provides for our scarcity, our need, our *not-enough* with His own life within us—His living water is the life and love of God.

To come is to believe and seek God.

- To drink is the reverent act of choosing, acknowledging, and receiving Christ in the present.
- To continually come and drink, is to live in the flow of the Holy Spirit.

More than a single action or just another task to add to the never-ending list of things we *should* do, abiding is an orientation of the heart.

For every thirst, for every need, and for every moment: believe and abide, remain and receive.

The apostle Paul declares, "I have been crucified with Christ; and it is no longer I who live, but Christ lives in me; and the *life* which I now live in the flesh I live by faith in the Son of God, who loved me and gave Himself up for me" (Galatians 2:20, emphasis added).

This *life we now live* includes what's happening in your life at this *now-moment*. Reading a book, taking a walk, driving the car, washing dishes, helping kids, presenting projects, answering questions—these are just a few of our daily opportunities for keeping company with Christ.

ABIDING IN OUR BUSY MOMENTS

Certain things just have to be done to maintain life and sanity. Not doing necessary tasks has a cost sooner or later. For instance, don't take out the trash, and it won't be too long before the house begins to stink. Decide that laundry isn't a priority and soon no one in the house has clean socks and underwear. See how that goes.

Our lives are filled up with busy. There are the goals we want to accomplish.

And the things we feel obligated to do.

And the things other people think we should do.

And the jobs others didn't do.

How about you? Do you find yourself squeezed in the time crunch, trying to find ways to stay connected with God in all you've got going?

Abiding with Jesus is walking in His Spirit, not walking after the flesh. Learning to keep company with Christ, we build the blessed habit of acknowledging Him in all our ways (Proverbs 3:6). I'd love to tell you that I've got this down and have mastered the art of abiding. But here's the reality check—I often run myself ragged, rushing through things and ignoring my thirst until my need becomes so great it will not be overlooked.

It's in the middle of the fray and the frantic that the choice to abide enables us to be filled with the resources of Christ. If abiding in Christ is relegated to church attendance or personal devotions, what do we do with the rest of life?

Consider these three simple ways to abide in Christ on a busy day:

1. Invite Jesus into your day. Start your day with a "Good morning, Lord." No matter how the day starts, we always have a choice to connect with our source of life. Here's what this looked like in my life last week: "Good morning, Lord. Please help me get moving," I pray with my head still on the pillow. By the time I force my feet out of bed, I'm running late. God reminds me that I have a choice to take a minute to invite God to go with me into the hurry.

2. Ask Jesus to express His life in you and believe He will do it. As I get dressed, I pray, "Lord, thank You for abiding in me today; help me to abide in You. I rely on Your strength today. Help me to stay mentally connected to You. Express Yourself through me as I teach my classes. I'm trusting You for everything I need as we do this day together." This is a snippet of life that replays frequently as I'm learning to keep company with God throughout my day.

3. Stop and ask God for what you need in the moment. Just this afternoon, I was frazzled and overwhelmed, caught among the tension of a deadline, the activity of family, and the mess in the house. I stopped and prayed, "Lord, this isn't how I want to feel. I'm going to rely on You. Show me what to focus on first."

Simple things can make a big difference. Ask Jesus to show you practical ways to rely on Him throughout your day. Expect Him to give you little reminders and nudges in the moment. Trust Jesus to guide and help you learn to abide in Him.

GOD'S LOVE IS HOME
FOR YOUR HEART

Making the choice to abide in Christ isn't merely an activity or a spiritual skill to master. Although it takes effort and growth on our part, God helps us develop a wholehearted habit that can become a natural part of our lives.

Jesus said, "If anyone loves Me, he will keep My word; and My Father will love him, and We will come to him and make Our abode with him" (John 14:23). As we learn to abide, the atmosphere of our moments changes because God's love is home for our hearts.

Moving has been a routine part of my married life as a military spouse. New orders. New place. New home. So there's something about inhabiting God's love that resonates with me.

On moving day, the truck pulls up to our new house that's just an address but not yet a home. Burly men haul furniture and boxes into the house. *What if they just left our belongings in the driveway or on the front porch?* I know this seems like a silly question, but how often have we lived on the side yards and the front porches of our relationship with God, rather than fully living at home in Him?

We unload and unpack. Put away and arrange. We sleep in the beds and eat in the kitchen. As we live there, our new house becomes our home, a secure place we live life in and from. In the midst of all our doing, we always return home, knowing that home is far more than an address.

Houses are made to live in, but the love of God is home for our hearts. So let me ask you a personal question: Are you hanging out on the edges of your relationship with God, or are you dwelling in His love? When you're at home, you become secure in God's love, and you don't have to wonder if you're in the right house or if you're really wanted.

Learning to keep company with Christ, we build the sacred habit of acknowledging Him in all our ways (Proverbs 3:6).

ABIDING TRAINS US TO TRUST GOD'S HEART IN HARD TIMES

"Problems are God's main tool for bringing us to the end of our own resources and into the deep experience of all His riches."[3] For me the most difficult time to abide in Christ is when problems create obstacles.

Some problems aren't just little irritations of a too-busy life.

Developing the holy habit of abiding prepares us to practice the presence of God rather than the persistence of our problems. The more secure we are in the love of God, the more we trust His heart even in the difficulties and disappointments of life.

My daughter is sixteen now. She gets out of the car with tears in her eyes. "My shoulder is killing me!" The words come tumbling out with a break in her voice. These are tears of frustration and discouragement, for I know my girl is brave about pain. During varsity volleyball tryouts in a large, competitive high school, she had a flare-up of an injury that we had hoped was better.

"Coach is going to keep me on the JV team because of my shoulder. I'm the *only* junior to not move up. Now I'll never know if I was good enough to make it," she tells me. She's worked for years to prepare for this day, to be ready, to be competitive. In reality, her adolescent identity has become tied up in playing volleyball.

I've had plenty of problems of my own, but my girl's disappointment sets off my anxiety meter, unsettling my heart. Silently I ask, "Why, God? Volleyball means so much to her, and she's worked so hard." Often our first response is to question God and focus on the problem, right? When we aren't abiding in Christ, suspicion comes easily as our hearts doubt the goodness of God in the midst of the challenge.

HELP FOR OUR HARD MOMENTS

Life has no shortage of trials. They come in all shapes and sizes. Your hard moments are different from mine, but we face the same temptation to let our emotions overshadow faith. The pressure of problems tempts us to react in the old ways we've learned to cope (flesh). Abiding protects our hearts when we need it most.

Stop over-focusing on the problem. Holiness comes when we look to God, discovering His view of the issue. This morning, I react with the go-to of my flesh—I get anxious because I can't make it all better with a Band-Aid and a kiss.

With the fragile self-esteem of a sixteen-year-old, will she listen to the taunts of the enemy endlessly nagging, "You're not good enough"? Will she define herself in the disdain of unkind girls? Will this cause her to believe she is *the one who didn't make it* in the larger things of life? These are the scenarios I create with my concern. Here's the truth: practicing the presence of problems creates issues rather than solves them.

"You've got to stop wondering how she'll come through; she's going to be fine. Every child has to face setbacks. You're an overreacting worrywart," I lecture myself (I'm good at that). With each rewind of the worry-tape in my head the problem grew, and the parameters of the issue expanded from today into the next.

Remember God is your very present help. As I fretted through my prayers for my daughter, the Holy Spirit brought these words to mind: "God is our refuge and strength, a very present help in trouble. . . . There is a river whose streams make glad the city of God, the holy dwelling place of the Most High. God is in the midst of her, she will not be moved" (Psalm 46:1, 4-5a).

God reminded me He's with me *in the midst of* the hurt and the disappointment. It's time to lean into Him rather than resist and resent. The more we've learned to abide in Christ, the more readily we receive His resources on our tough days.

Trusting God fuels faith on the problem days, whatever the size of the challenge. Otherwise, this is all just nice religious talk with no substance. God is in the midst of me, and He is in you, always present and ever faithful. Stay connected; don't let this habit go in the pressure of the moment.

Focusing on the problem blinds us to God's presence and impacts our experience. Consumed with our problems, we can easily be so focused on solving issues that we don't recognize God's provisions in the midst of the trial.

Practicing the presence of problems is striving, the most exhausting work of all. "'Cease striving and know that I am God'" (Psalm 46:10). Discovering the holy art of abiding has everything to do with knowing God in the midst of our pain. "The LORD of hosts is with us: the God of Jacob is our stronghold" (Psalm 46:11).

Cease striving is often translated as "be still." The Hebrew word for "be still" is *raphah*, meaning "to sink, relax, sink down, let drop." It also means to let down your hand and to desist from any person or thing. For me, the translation is simple: STOP WORRYING!

Are you ready to stop the striving and the battling, the controlling and the fixing that your problems can provoke? What's holding you back from *dwelling in* the loving presence of God rather than *dwelling on* your circumstances? *On* or *in*—abiding enables us to leap the God-sized gap between the two.

Oh friend, sink into a quiet place of inner stillness that has laid down every self-effort, resentment, and false source of strength. This is the two-fold command:

Be still.

And

Know that I am God.

What difference can one abiding choice to be still make? It is in a posture of abiding that the streams of God's presence calm our hearts, and we can know that He *really* is our God most high, our God right now.

SIMPLE WAYS TO PRACTICE GOD'S PRESENCE

1. Remember your goal is to trust in Christ, not control or fix every problem. The beautiful byproduct of abiding helps us be more present with others as well. A few weeks later, my daughter and I sat on the back porch. We talked about how she was feeling and how she was handling disappointment. She told me it was hard and it felt awkward, frustrating, and discouraging. Realizing I don't have to have all the answers, God is teaching me the power of "presence."

2. Work on the habit of talking with Jesus and include Him in your thoughts. As I chatted with my daughter, I silently prayed, a simple habit of "knowing" God in the moment. "Lord, help me encourage her. Let this be a setback lasting for a moment rather than a message resonating for a lifetime. She's at such a tender age for building confidence. Help us both to trust you in disappointment."

After days of fretting about the problem, something internal settled as I made the choice to trust His heart. I may not have known what would happen next, but I knew the One who was leading the way.

3. Recognize God's encouragement as you work through problems. From the top of the porch, a little bird fell, landing a few feet away from us. Still and stunned, he seemed to look at us with a direct stare, eyes unblinking. "Do you think he can fly? Is he hurt?" my daughter asked with concern.

I reflected on my concerns for my own little bird, the one who wants to jump high, run fast, and spike hard—the one I want to soar in life. The sparrow hopped around a bit before allowing us to guide him off the porch to fly away to his next adventure. Some call this a God-moment, and it was. My eyes were opened to God's gift of a tangible reminder that this problem will not hinder my daughter from taking flight again soon.

Here are a few things I didn't know at the time. A few weeks later, she had an ankle injury that took her out for the season. I didn't know team relationships were toxic and unhealthier than any physical injury. She began working for her physical therapist, who encouraged her interest in medicine. And I had no idea God would rebuild her confidence by working with adult clients. God answered the true concerns of my heart with unexpected answers. One of the blessings of abiding is the gift of noticing He is with you in the midst of it all. I realize that, too often, I've focused on a specific answer and completely missed the joy of seeing God work in the midst of the problem.

A sacred glimpse of God's heart lets me see that just as His eye is on the sparrow, His eye is on my sweet girl.

4. Learn to redefine a good day from doing to being. Forgiven, accepted, remade with love, we are learning the holy habit of abiding. Change your experience by shifting your definition of a good day as one where you stay connected to Christ and receive everything you need to . . .

Be present.
Be dependent.
Be filled.
Be loved.
Be home.
Be helped.
Be healed.

Spiritual growth comes down to the life we live each moment. Abiding is the only way to live holy in the moment. There's no other way. *It's that simple, Holy Girl.*

SIMPLE REMINDERS TO ABIDE

- Abiding begins with God's invitation to "come and drink" from His presence.
- For every thirst, for every need, and for every moment: abide, believe, stay, remain, and receive.
- Walking in Jesus' spirit happens when you are depending on Him; walking after the flesh is when you don't.
- God's love is home for your heart. Abiding trains you to trust God's heart on your hard days.
- Practicing the presence of problems creates problems rather than solves them.
- Stop over-focusing on the problem. Remember God is your very present help.
- Focusing on the problem blinds you to God's presence and impacts your experience.
- Work on the habit of talking with Jesus and include Him in your thoughts.

CHAPTER 5

MOMENTS TO SURRENDER

Commitment is what I am promising to do for God. Surrender is placing myself and my life in His hands to do with as He pleases.

—Bob George, *Classic Christianity*

Though holiness rests in the daily choices we make, days quickly turn into years. Holiness also moves through seasons of our lives, transitions and changes packaged in big moments as well as small ones. As we build a lifestyle of abiding, God is always at work, growing our hearts closer to Him.

Sometimes big changes barge in unannounced. One minute is normal, everyday routine; the next opens the door to something you never saw coming.

In our blindsided moments, holiness isn't always our first thought, our instinctive choice. At least it's a struggle for me. One night as we linger over empty dinner plates, I'm feeling mopey about the new empty spot at the table. Our daughter left for college two weeks ago, and my heart is still tender. My husband says, "There's a ministry position open in Pensacola. These jobs don't come open very often, and I really want to do this. What do you think?"

Totally unprepared for this unexpected change of plans, I look around at the house we bought to retire in. After all the years of military moves, we bought a place to put down roots. A place our kids could call home and come back to. In a blink, what had seemed certain isn't certain anymore.

I can't answer right away. My head spins, desperately trying to process the situation, what it means, how I feel, and it all pushes against what I know

I *should* say. With conflict in my heart, I just want to wail loud and long, "Noooooooo!"

UNWILLING AND RESISTANT

Don't mess with me—don't change the plan! This deal wasn't on the table.

I thought getting out of the military would bring an end to the struggle of my flesh pattern of anxiety triggered by moving. Apparently not.

I can't do it again.

I won't.

I don't deserve this.

It's my turn.

What about me?

My inner crazy ramps up in an instant, blaring in my head even as I know that I *should* be willing to talk about it.

I *should* be excited that after twenty-four years of military service, my husband has found his dream job. And it's ministry, which is another big set of *shoulds*. I *should* be thrilled to serve God in ministry. I *should* be willing to move. I *should* be able to trust Him with having my girl twelve hours away instead of two.

I *should* have gotten over this transition anxiety by now.

But I haven't. And I can't. Not in this unexpected question. The worst part is this: I don't understand why I'm such a wreck. After a silent battle with myself, I finally answer, "Let's pray about it, go for the interview, and see what happens."

I don't say this in faith—I say it with hope of delaying a decision, hoping God will shut the door and let me off the hook. I know that's not a very godly attitude, but sometimes pressure hits out of the blue and we just react. This is the reactionary way of our flesh God wants to transform. Unwilling and resistant, what's buried in our heart erupts and gets out before we can reign it in and dress it up nice.

Knowing this is hard for me, my husband asks, "What's your main concern?" Along with my resistance to another move are several factors. Professionally, I'm tired of starting over, reestablishing my credibility every few years. Socially, I'm weary of the cycle of leaving support systems and making new friends. But my greatest concern is for our kids. We moved here two years ago when our daughter Grace was a junior in high school. We watched our sunny extrovert struggle to find her place and make her way. Not wanting to live far from home, she intentionally chose a college two hours away. *How can I leave knowing this?*

"I feel like we'd be ripping the rug out from under Grace to move so far away before she's even settled in school. It's only been two weeks. And then there's Natalie; we'll go through another hard transition with a teenager. I love the idea of a ministry job, but the timing just feels wrong. It's too soon." (Translation: *This isn't my timing!*)

Ten days later we flew to Florida ready to interview, which took place over a weekend. By this time, I've spent hours on my face, pressing my nose in the carpet, begging God to remove my anxiety so I can willingly embrace this change in my plans. So I can be free and whole-hearted to support my man and follow my God.

During the weekend, I'm a mixed up, wigged-out mess of some strange combination of *want-to*, *should-do*, and *afraid-to*. Seems like my inner wimp always barges in when I most want to be strong. And I hate myself like this. I don't want to be the woman who's hanging on by a thread. Truth is, this deep resistance is both a wound and a shame holding me captive in more ways than I realize.

I try my best to be authentic, positive, and honest. "Yes, I'm struggling with anxiousness about moving again, but it'll pass. I don't want it to hold us back."

In private, my husband hurts for me, wanting to help and trying to understand. Moving has never been as hard for him. He looks at me with a question in his eyes, "Honey, this is almost like you've got PTSD. Why is this so hard for you?" With the clarity of turning on a light, I know he's right. *Why have I ignored the problem for so long?*

BROKENNESS IS A PROCESS LEADING TO SURRENDER

We've had four cross-country and international moves since heading to California in 2000, the one that nearly broke me. Each transition has been an emotional and physical battle zone, as debilitating anxiety resurfaced with every move. What began with a physical syndrome seemed to rewire entrenched pathways in my brain. Because it was mostly associated with moving, I plodded through, knowing I'd eventually settle down. I kept hoping I would mature beyond this phase of my Christian life by increased faith, regular Bible study, and diligent service.

If my kids struggled like this, I would have sought help. *Why haven't I done this for myself? Why have I kept sweeping the problem under the rug, and how has fear gotten such a grip on me?*

Sometimes holiness comes with a question—a question turning us to God in a deeper way. A question that opens our closed minds to be willing to talk about our deep struggles. This question was a hungry-hearted choice to ask God to show me what my anxiety was really about. How about you? Is there a key flesh trait you can't get past? A hurt you've been unwilling to deal with or a pattern you've ignored and avoided?

There's something brave and sacred about staring straight at your deep struggles, ready to seek help, ready to stop denying the problems. Ready to surrender. So often we hold on to the very things keeping us stuck.

Now I understand God used the repeated pressure of moving to bring me to a point of readiness to surrender. Over the years, no amount of talking, listing pros and cons, repenting, or asking forgiveness conquered my fear and insecurity. I read books on overcoming anxiety. I memorized Scripture. I promised I would get myself together. All my best efforts could not banish my uneasiness.

When my proactive efforts didn't solve the problem, I started with shaming self-lectures. *What's wrong with me? Some faith I have. Worry is a sin. I'm holding my husband back, robbing him of his dream job.*

It's all my fault.

I called myself names like *dream-killer* and *undependable.* Listening to the whispered lies and harsh accusations of the enemy, I sank into a silent, secret hole of depression. I kept going on the outside, but inside I knew something was broken, with a wide disconnect between my faith and my emotions. All the things I wanted to be, hoped to be, felt I should be seemed scattered in pieces, while the *dis-ease* of my soul would not settle down.

THE BATTLE FOR CONTROL

We all have struggles gripping our souls, ones that threaten to undo us. Ones we keep faltering over, getting up to only fall again. Sins, self, addictions, flesh—call it what you will, the struggle is real, and it has a good purpose.

Yes, you read that correctly. God has a divine purpose in the struggles seeming to break us because that's exactly what they're designed to do. It's in our *nose-in-the-carpet* moments where we come face to face with the fact that we are not the answer.

We don't have the answer.

And we can't figure out the answer, even when we pull out the big guns and strategies that have worked in the past.

Maybe anxiety and fear aren't the dogs nipping at your heels. Your struggle may include other strategies such as outbursts, withdrawal, escapism, addiction, manipulation, or unforgiveness to name a few. Your challenge to surrender control may look very different from mine. Yet for all of us, there comes a time when God leads us into deeper brokenness by making the old ways—the self-help and pull-yourself-up-by-the-bootstraps ways—less productive. The road to brokenness is paved with bad news, difficult marriages, rebellious teens, poor health, runaway tempers, blocked goals, bad habits, rejection, or failure—tools in God's hands to weaken the ways we've learned to meet our needs with our own efforts.

In our deepest discouragements, hopeless heartbreaks, and worst messes, we finally see that overconfidence in self leads to conflict and frustration, a place of brokenness.

We all have our *must haves* and our *what about me*'s, needs and desires we believe we must fill in order to be OK in this life. These are the ways we've solved problems, garnered success, and avoided pain. Most of us have gotten pretty good at it too.

When we resort to the flesh, we want to control how the answers look, demanding things must be a certain way in order for us to be happy. For me, finding stability after years of moving was a "right" I felt I had earned through all my sacrifice and struggle.

These beliefs have a strange way of hardening into personal definitions and demands of how people should act: husbands *should* build us up, kids *should* respect us, and bosses *should* appreciate our hard work. Maybe the hardest are the often-unrecognized demands and rights we place upon ourselves:

I should stop feeling anxious.

I must succeed to prove my worth.

I can't make the same mistakes as my parents for my kids to turn out OK.

I need to be the perfect wife for my husband to be happy with me.

I must have approval of others to be OK.

I don't deserve to be treated like this.

I have earned this.

I'm entitled to a normal life.

And on and on it goes. The silent language of self-reliance mutters and accuses. We fight to control outcomes and secure needs through our own beliefs that are tied to what we're thinking. This is why it matters that we believe what is true. For sure, we usually don't say these beliefs aloud. Most of the time, we don't peel back the layers of our thoughts and emotions to see what lurks beneath the surface. And determined to succeed, to make life better, we scrape by with every scrap of self we can muster.

Our need to control our lives morphs and twists in the winds of our fears, demands, and rights. Living by our flesh, God's gifts harden into entitlements as gratitude tarnishes with expectations.

Where is holiness in this struggle? How do we choose holiness in our desperate dogfights to right the wrongs and gather the gains we deserve? Many times, we don't even see the struggle for what it is: a battle for control over our lives.

THE STRUGGLE TO SURRENDER OUR RIGHTS

Talking with my husband as we waited for an answer about the ministry job in Pensacola, I laid down my right to live the life I'd pictured, the one I thought I had to have. I was ready. Willing to say yes. Surely this meant we would get the job and make the move. When we got the news the job had been offered to another couple, I felt so confused.

Why all this angst to not get the job? Did we lose this chance due to my anxiety, because I couldn't fully trust God in this area of my life? Wasn't the point of surrender to move into this new place of ministry? I instinctively made this challenge a pass or fail test of doing the right thing. I think God was more interested in showing me how tightly I was clinging to my rights.

When the bottom drops out and things are falling apart, we have one holy choice that can change everything—the choice to surrender our rights to God. Our most sacred gift is our right to surrender our independence, the one thing truly ours to give.

Surrender is sacred territory of the soul, and talking about it comes easier in smaller issues of life. But there comes a time, set by God, when the choice to surrender our rights involves a deep struggle to release what we've been afraid to let go, the things we've built our world around, things that cannot satisfy.

In our brokenness, we ignore parts of ourselves bound to sins, hindered by self-focus and false motives, and burdened by lies, hurt, and guilt. For years, I had ignored deep anxiety of my soul balking at the uncertainty of each transition in life. Jesus revealed how deeply I, like the woman at the well, sought contentment and security in ways that just didn't work.

What does surrender look like for some of the women I know? For Kris, it's letting go of resentment that she's slowly losing her mother to dementia. It's trusting God with her mom in the midst of her decline. For Larissa, surrender is choosing daily gratitude even while her husband fights terminal cancer. For Sarah, it's releasing her rights to have her husband act the way she'd like, knowing her value comes from Christ. For Susan, it's trusting God with her son's severe allergy to bee stings. For Rebecca, it's trusting God with her career when bypassed for promotion. Each one of these women trusts God, letting go of their *must haves* and *what about me's*.

When God brings us to a place of brokenness, we lay down guilt and shame in the holy rhythms of confession, repentance, and forgiveness as we finally realize our strategies are unproductive. Brokenness is the path to the holy ground of surrendering control and trusting that God *really* is good and that He *really* does know what's best. Surrender prays alongside of Christ, "Not My will, but Yours be done" (Luke 22:42).

THE HOLY CHOICE TO RECEIVE LIKE A CHILD

Surrender opens the door to receive the fullness of God. Consider the interesting contrast between children and a rich man's questions in Mark 10.

Jesus said, "Permit the children to come to Me; do not hinder them; for the kingdom of God belongs to such as these. Truly I say to you, whoever does not receive the kingdom of God like a child will not enter it *at all*. And He took them in His arms and *began* blessing them, laying His hands on them" (vv. 14-16, emphasis added).

Faith like a child, simple and pure—this is a choice we all have every day. Not needing to know it all or have it all, children aren't trying to prove themselves to Christ. They don't hold back, afraid Jesus will force them to do something they don't want to do. They simply, joyfully come. We all need childlike faith to receive the kingdom of God.

Can you choose to be like the child in the arms of Jesus today? Will you let Him bless you? Have you wondered about this blessing Jesus gives the children? One of the meanings of the word *blessing* is to consecrate with a prayer, to ask God's blessings. It also means "to speak well of, to prosper, to make happy, to be favored of God."

One simple thing for today, one holy thing for your heart, is to rest in His arms and let Jesus bless you as you receive His kingdom, His heart, and His will. Open hands and hearts are ready to receive. We often see surrender as giving up, but more importantly, it is the blessing of receiving, safe in the love of God.

A shift of perspective from losing my rights to gaining Christ's life makes all the difference. Rather than the language of loss, surrender is the way of love that leads to freedom. See what I mean as you read the next story.

THE HOLY HABIT OF RECOGNIZING OUR SELF-RIGHTEOUSNESS

Shortly after Jesus blessed the children, a rich man ran to Jesus, asking, "What shall I do to inherit eternal life?" When Jesus told him to obey the law, the man replied, "Teacher, I have kept all these things from my youth up" (Mark 10:17, 20).

This man has done it all right. Every single bit. Every single day.

Sounds great, doesn't it? Haven't we all, in some way, wanted to be the one who gets it all right, to make everything all right? And yet, something's missing; he still felt he wasn't doing enough.

This man asked the question the flesh always asks, *What shall I do?*

Poieo, the Greek word for "what shall I do," is also translated as "to work or perform." To act rightly, do well, and perform to a promise are also bound up in this concept.

What shall I do? Isn't this the wrong question? **Sometimes holiness is as simple as asking the right question.** Taking his righteousness on himself (trying to get himself right), the man can only see something he must do in order to draw closer to God. Isn't this our problem as well when we try to get ourselves right with our own abilities, looks, and successes? Here's the problem of self-righteousness, this getting-ourselves-right way of living—it's never enough, and we're never sure, never free, and never at rest.

Knowing what the man really needed, Jesus looked with love rather than reprimand. "'One thing you lack: go and sell all you possess and give to the poor, and you will have treasure in heaven; and come, follow Me.' But at these words he was saddened, and he went away grieving, for he was one who owned much property" (Mark 10:21-22).

How fair is that? Looking at this situation from the rules of fair play, we don't understand this answer. The disciples didn't get it either. Jesus isn't giving the man an impossible task to struggle with on his own. He's not setting him up for failure and defeat. What if Jesus simply wanted the man to recognize his dependence on himself when he loved and trusted in money more than God?

Struggling with my fears for our future plans, I wrote in my journal, "Lord, I feel like you've set me up for failure." I thought I had come with my need for security only to receive an impossible answer of another move, that is, God isn't really good. *I can't do this again.* Later, in the silence of a sleepless night, God answered my question. I still remember the moonlight reaching through the frosted window in the bathroom. Yes, sometimes God speaks when we're on the potty—how holy is that?

I have not set you up to fail; I have set you up to grow.

I don't think Jesus set this man up to fail either. The reality is this—sometimes it's impossible by design, impossible on purpose. Not to keep us out but to usher us in because surrender is the only way we can come deeper into the life of God.

What if our riches aren't merely money in the bank? Jesus spoke to the man's real need—to stop hoarding wealth, to stop building an identity and a life on what he could accumulate and accomplish. This is the challenge and the blessed choice of surrender. Just as Jesus revealed his lack—the wealth of the rich man—His eye is on the thing we treasure most. The one thing we've built our confidence and security on, the thing we cringe to even bring into the conversation.

I don't know what's in your life bank, but I know this: we all face this hard and holy choice to surrender the wealth of our self-reliance. It's so easy to view this story through the lens of a harsh God. Suspicion defines a God who takes away and requires the hardest route. Have you viewed God with distrust? When you're afraid to surrender, remember how easily the children were blessed.

Jesus explained to his disciples, "How hard it will be for those who are wealthy to enter the kingdom of God!"

"Who then can be saved?" they ask with astonishment (Luke 18:26).

This is the struggle of surrender; it feels backwards, cutting against the grain—dying to live, losing to gain, first to be last. We can't receive the riches of God when we store up our value through our efforts, possessions, or abilities.

WHAT WILL WE CHOOSE?

The man left sad, shoulders slouched, and broken inside. He couldn't let go of all the treasure, pride, value, worth, comfort, and identity. His treasure was how he knew himself, as a rich man, and his identity enmeshed with the thing he couldn't give away. To give away his possessions was to give away himself, and that can feel like a terrifying, impossible request if we haven't learned to trust God with the faith of a child.

The contrast of these two stories opens something tender in my soul as I recognize the root of my struggles. I see the choice: I respond like a child who runs to Jesus, empty-handed and excited to enjoy His presence. To trust like a child is a choice, simple and holy. Or I can live with the erroneous belief like the rich man did, that I can come to Christ with my good religious track record, seeking to do one more thing to bring me closer and make me more worthy, while holding on to my treasure with an iron grip that smothers my soul.

Looking in the mirror at the intense anxiety of another move, I realize I've hoarded security with my *must haves* and my *what about me*'s. I've stored up approval trying to do it all right, and anxiety reveals my fear that I'm going to lose what has become so important.

Like the rich man, I can seek Jesus from the grid of what I must do, should do, didn't do, or can't do, missing His heart and missing the point.

And missing myself.

Have you felt the impossible breaking something inside? Have your false towers of pride, security, control, and identity begun to crumble? Surrender comes by way of the broken road.

Breaking down lies we've believed and things we've convinced ourselves we must have, Jesus breaks the hold of the things we can't let go. He breaks up the ground of our hard, needy hearts and breaks us out of the traps keeping us captive. He is an all-things-are-possible God who breaks us free.

Free to surrender.
Free to release our rights.
Free to receive His truth.
Free to rest in His arms.

What will you choose in the holy hush of this moment, in the dawning light of fresh understanding? Could you make a sacred choice to change your perspective? Rather than seeing yourself as a sinner in the hands of an angry God, you are a cherished child in the arms of a God who loves you deeply. When you struggle with your impossible moments (and we all do), remember this prayer of the apostle Paul: "that in everything you were enriched [made wealthy] . . . in all speech and all knowledge . . . so that you are not lacking in any gift, awaiting eagerly the revelation of our Lord Jesus Christ, who will also confirm you to the end, blameless in the day of our Lord Jesus Christ" (1 Corinthians 1:5-8).

What are we afraid to let go of or to let loose? to admit or confess? to repent or forgive? Unlike the children who run freely into the arms of Jesus, the rich man couldn't see his wealth as his spiritual lack. To him, to me, and to you, what is this gift that is big enough to make us enough? This gift of Living Water for every need?

Charisma, favor received without any merit of our own, is divine grace explained as the gifts of faith, knowledge, holiness, and virtue. *Charisma* is received due to the power of divine grace operating in the soul by the Holy Spirit.[1] This gift blows the doors off every prison cell and gives us everything we need to entrust our hearts fully to God.

Surrender isn't a one-time act—get it over and done with, like eating spinach or taking medicine.

Learning to live from an attitude of surrender is a sacred approach to daily life, this present now. Letting go of our rights is an action, an orientation of our heart, and an attitude of our will by cooperating with God who is putting us together, holy and whole.

We're choosing holy, choosing surrender, our deepest act of loving God. God's grace is the gift that makes us rich, not lacking in anything we need to overcome our fears of falling short, being left out or left behind, failing to reach the goal or pass the finish line. Our fears of being inferior, needy, wanting, lacking in excellence and worth are answered when we receive the holiness of *charisma.* In the letting go of self, we gain God's more-than-enough miracle of grace that brings rest for our souls. *Friend, surrender is a gift of holy for your heart.*

SIMPLE REMINDERS TO SURRENDER

- Brokenness makes you realize the methods of your flesh don't work.
- Breaking down the lies you've believed and the things you've convinced yourself you must have, Jesus breaks the hold of the things you can't let go.
- Letting go of control over your life is a vital part of surrender.

- Trusting God with your deep needs enables you to release your rights.
- Brokenness is the path leading you to the holy ground of surrendering control and trusting that God really is good and He really does know what's best for you.
- Recognize that self-righteousness hinders surrender.
- *What shall I do?* isn't the right question for surrender.
- Surrender is the only way you can come deeper into the life of God.
- Learning to live from an attitude of surrender is a spiritual approach to daily life.

CHAPTER 6

MOMENTS TO REST

Let the life of Christ set you free from a rushing life that has no
time for rest or the enjoyment of family, His creation, and most
of all Him!

—Michael Wells, *Problems, God's Presence & Prayer*

"What would you do with free time if you had it?"

The question takes us all by surprise, as if it were some strange, unfamiliar
concept. Maybe even a foreign language. It makes us think. And remember.
And wish.

"I can't remember the last time I had an afternoon to myself. Free time?
I wouldn't even know what to do with it anymore," Angie sighs as she leans
back in her chair.

"I know, right," commiserates another friend. "Since my baby was born, I
haven't even been able to drink an entire cup of coffee. I'm so tired these days,
I need the caffeine now more than ever."

"We had a free evening last night, and I fell asleep on the couch. I'm too
tired to enjoy time to relax when I have it," chimed in someone else.

By this time, we're on a roll as the question has hit a nerve. If you were
sitting at the table with us, I bet you could jump into the conversation with
your own frustrations with how responsibilities, life management, and work
pile up with lightning speed.

We all need time for our souls to breathe and our bodies to rest as chronic busyness is just a normal day in today's world. Pressured by culture, we've swallowed the lie that a busy life is a fulfilling life. More is better, faster is sooner, as if frantic is the new holiness.

But like a frayed, tattered sweater, we wear the warning signs that our driving activity has a taxing cost:

- We trudge and plod, just trying to make it through the day.
- Racing against the tyranny of the clock, we sacrifice the important for the urgent again and again.
- Bombarded with guilt and frustration, we default to thinking we must somehow work harder to get ourselves together.

What would you add to this list?

When we are exhausted and stressed, our vision narrows to near-sighted—we only see as far as the next task, next event, or next due date. I'm not pointing any fingers, just telling you what happens to me. Actually my hands are too full to be able to point my finger at anyone. *If I let go of this load, I'm going to drop it.*

When we're tired, it affects our body, soul, and spirit. Disjointed. Disgruntled. Disenchanted. . . . Oh, how it weighs heavily on the soul, this tiredness seeping into our lives.

When is the last time you rested and didn't feel guilty about it?

We struggle and strain under burdens of hectic days, unfinished work, tense relationships, unmet goals, and countless other challenges. Why do we feel selfish when we take time to rest and refresh? As if rest is a luxury we can't afford?

The truth is that we can't afford not to rest. Today, give yourself room to breathe. You may just find this one simple thing opens more space in your life for God to move.

FIVE SIMPLE WAYS TO FIND REST FOR YOUR BODY

Try a few of these simple ideas for physical rest.

- Invite Jesus to evaluate your commitments and simplify your schedule. Let Him show you how to create margin. Jot down any ideas He brings to mind.
- Pray and plan before accepting new commitments so you don't overload your schedule.
- Commit to getting enough sleep. For one week make bedtime a priority and note the difference adequate rest makes.
- Pace yourself. Give yourself permission to stop and rest when you need to.
- Plan ahead for especially busy seasons so they don't catch you off guard and unprepared.

SABBATH IS GOD'S DESIGN FOR REST

Choosing holiness in the moment, we discover a better way, the resting way of deep-down trust in the goodness of God. Have you considered how rest can be a holy thing? Does Sabbath seem like an unrelated concept for modern life? Actually I don't think we've ever needed it more! For the weary and the worn, for the holy and the hardworking, rest is a choice, but it's also a sacred command.

God doesn't take rest lightly. "For in six days the LORD made the heavens and the earth . . . and rested on the seventh day; therefore the LORD blessed the Sabbath day and made it holy" (Exodus 20:11).

Holy. Sacred. Set apart. A day unlike other work-filled days. Honoring the Sabbath is a command with a penalty of death in the Old Testament (Exodus 31:14). I'm thankful this is no longer the case, but the reality check is this:

there's a destructive cost to neglecting rest. When we sand our souls thin with endless physical, mental, emotional, or spiritual toil, it breeds a kind of restlessness in our hearts.

John Ortberg writes of the hurried soul, "It means to be so preoccupied with myself and my life that I am unable to be fully present with God, with myself, and with other people."[1]

Busy schedules left unchecked create harried souls that are preoccupied, spiritually drained, disengaged with people, and distant from God.[2] Without rest, we don't have harmony, feeling an increasing disconnect between our body, soul, spirit, and our God.

Mark Buchanan explains the rest of God in a way that opens a new perspective: "But without rest, we miss the rest of God: the rest he invites us to enter more fully so that we might know him more deeply. . . . Sabbath is both a day and an attitude to nurture such stillness. It is both time on a calendar and a disposition of the heart. It's a day we enter, but just as much a way we see. Sabbath imparts the rest of God—actual physical, mental, spiritual rest, but also the *rest* of God—the things of God's nature and presence we miss in our busyness."[3]

Been there, done that? I think we all have.

Friend, put your feet up and stop to consider how you can honor and protect Sabbath in your heart, as well as in your schedule. If you could do anything you wanted, what is one creative way you'd love to savor Sabbath rest? Pray about fresh ways to celebrate God and enjoy rest, writing down the ideas God brings to mind. Over the next few weeks, make an intentional choice to give these ideas a try.

SABBATH IS PERMISSION TO CARE FOR YOUR SOUL

I don't want to oversimplify Sabbath, but what if God's command to rest is also divine permission to care for our souls? Remember the story Jesus told:

"A certain woman named Martha received him into her house. And she had a sister called Mary, which also sat at Jesus' feet, and heard his word. But Martha was cumbered about much serving" (Luke 10:38-40 KJV).

Some days I'm a Martha. I can *Martha* myself into a frenzy, wielding my to-do list like a weapon. Though *cumbered* isn't a word we use much anymore, we live its meaning all too easily on days when our tasks outnumber time and energy. *Cumbered*, used this one time in Scripture, means to be over-occupied or too busy about a thing.

I feel Martha's good intentions. So often my want-to-do-the-good-thing clashes with the reality of my time and energy. With the grace of hospitality, Martha welcomes Jesus into her home. The pressure of preparations to please and maybe impress, turn an opportunity into an obligation. A gift into an expectation.

Martha's desire to serve plays out with high expectations of both herself and others. *Oh yes, I know this problem all too well. Do you?*

While Martha is seasoning the sauce and setting the table, she spies Mary who "also sat at Jesus' feet, and heard His word." What does Martha do? Complain, of course!

Get irritated? Yes.

Manipulate to fix the problem? Umm . . . that too: "Lord, tell her to help me and do her part" (Luke 10:40 AMP).

When we feel worried and bothered with much serving and work, we often feel entitled to have others meet our expectations. After all, we're sacrificing our time and effort to do the good thing of serving others. The least everyone else can do is appreciate our hard work and help out. *I'm pretty sure there isn't a woman on the planet who can't relate to this situation.*

Jesus said to a frantic and frazzled Martha—the one I know—the one trying to get it all done and get it all right: "Martha, Martha, you are worried and bothered about so many things; but only one thing is necessary, for Mary has chosen the good part, which shall not be taken away from her" (Luke 10:41).

There's something about this conversation between Jesus and Martha that tempts us to want to take sides—Martha was wrong and Mary was right. Either you sit at Jesus' feet like Mary or you work with Martha's nagging. Yet think back to the beginning of this story, "Mary, which *also* sat at Jesus' feet, and heard his word" (Luke 10:39 KJV, emphasis added).

There's one very important but very small word we haven't mentioned: also.

The power of *also*.

Mary is *also-ing*—she was working, but she also made time to sit and listen when she had the opportunity to enjoy the Lord's presence. Pouring out and taking time to refill. This rhythm sets our hearts straight as we grasp the truth that time with Christ is not only the better thing but also the necessary thing.

Haven't we learned this the hard way? And for some crazy reason, we keep learning the same lesson—not because we're slow learners but because this is the necessary thing.

It's that important.

Martha works hard with good intent, serving Christ but neglecting what she needs in order to sustain life in her work. When we separate work from worship, sacred from secular, faith life from real life, we feel pressured to choose between the spiritual and the practical.

There's so much more to this story than a lesson on time management and priorities. Mary shows us a position of the heart—quiet, seated, listening, and present—making the most of the opportunity to learn from Christ.

"But you, when you pray, go into your inner room, close your door and pray to your Father who is in secret, and your Father who sees what is done in secret will reward you" (Matthew 6:6). Sacred secrecy takes place in our inner room, our inmost heart, present and intimate with Christ. This is our holy of holies.

Soul rest is inner-room living in a busy world.

What if your inner room is a condition of the heart, rather than a space on the schedule, a place in the house, or a formula for spiritual growth?

For so long, I thought time with God had to be a certain way with a specific time and formula. It had to be quiet, with everything else stopped and put away. Too often, quiet didn't happen.

And I felt guilty.

I felt lacking and displeasing to God.

I felt like a spiritual failure, as if I had to do everything just so.

What if we learn to be present WITH GOD in the midst of busy times as well as the quiet moments? What if we learn the secret of inner-room living WITH GOD, rather than working for God? This is the practical power of sacred choices.

Believe. Choose. Love. Abide. Surrender. Rest. These are our necessary things, holy choices teaching us to learn, pray, speak, work, rest, and play with God—no lines and no divisions between sacred and secular, between doing and being.

JESUS TEACHES US HOW TO FIND REST OUR SOUL CRAVES

Rest and work. Work and rest. Work isn't just about jobs, meetings, shopping, cleaning, or carpooling—physical work of the body. There's also the work of the soul. This is the labor fraying our inward seams with our soul's struggle to feel loved, valued, worthy, accepted, and secure—needs and fears that disturb peace and unravel emotions.

Unmet needs sneak into conversations and motivations, twisting good intentions into coping ways of our flesh. We work harder to meet standards, gain approval, and find success. *What if I'm really not enough? How can I prove my value and secure acceptance in my relationships? Surely God won't be happy with me until I become more or do more....* What are the questions your weary soul asks?

Without faith, love, and surrender, the work of trying to make our soul OK is an exhausting, relentless toil of self-effort. Truly, our greatest struggles are to manage self, working to do whatever it takes to feel all right.

Know what? This is the struggle of self-righteousness—trying to make ourselves right apart from God. This is the war our flesh wages against our spirit, leaving us weary and wounded on battlefields of independence and self-effort.

Too often, we twist holiness into self-imposed molds of perfectionism dressed up for Sunday and lurking behind our efforts to please God.

For all our weary-hearted moments, Jesus invites us to experience rest for our souls: "Come to Me, all who are weary and heavy-laden, and I will give you rest. Take My yoke upon you and learn from Me, for I am gentle and humble in heart, and you will find rest for your souls. For my yoke is easy and my burden is light" (Matthew 11:28-30).

Learning from Jesus is to learn by experience, to be in the habit of or be accustomed to. What burdens do you carry? Today is your day to rest in Christ. Pray this verse and give Him your concerns, rest your problems against His strength.

TEN SIMPLE WAYS TO FIND RESTS FOR YOUR SOUL

Consider a few of these ways to let Christ teach you His way of rest:

1. Ask God to examine your heart, and confess any sin He reveals.

2. Trust God with the people you care about.

3. Is there anyone you need to forgive? Unforgiveness *really* is poison to your soul.

4. Pray, "Lord, what do You want me to know about this burden/situation?"

5. What ways are you trying to control things you cannot control? How can you release them to God?

6. Are there situations or relationships where you are taking responsibility that isn't yours to bear? Entrust them to Christ.

7. Ask Jesus to help you learn how to rest in pressure, conflict, or uncertainty.

8. Rest the outcomes of your efforts in God's capable hands and release the stress of performance.

9. Intentionally express your love for God throughout the day.

10. Release your preconceptions and live in expectancy as you stay in the moment with Christ.

Which of these suggestions struck a chord with you? What would it look like for you to act on one simple thing? What would choosing rest look like in your situation?

As Jesus teaches you how to rest, find freedom from your burdens of sin, shame, fear, and self-righteousness by taking hold of the truth that you are forgiven, cleansed, and made new. Holy rest is trusting Jesus to walk with you, helping you and teaching you every step of the way.

REST YOUR SPIRIT IN THE RIGHTEOUSNESS OF GOD

Spiritual rest is the great relief of realizing we no longer have to work at keeping the law with the blood and sweat of our own goodness. Our efforts matter, but we are made righteous by our new birth in Christ rather than our behavior. Though we sin and get ourselves into all kinds of issues, we have forgiveness because God has taken care of our sins in Christ. "He made Him who knew no sin on our behalf, so that we might become the righteousness of God in Him" (2 Corinthians 5:21).

Do you believe this? For real? Do you see yourself the way God sees you as righteous? You may have heard a common phrase in Christian lingo: "I'm just a sinner saved by grace." However, according to 2 Corinthians 5:21, it is more accurate to say something like, "I'm not who I once was—I once was a sinner, but now I'm righteous, a saint, a new creation with a new identity." Now you have a new identity, a new-creation self (2 Corinthians 5:17). You are holy. Sometimes you'll sin, but that's no longer who you are. Remember, your identity is not your behavior. Embracing this truth brings the best kind of rest for your spirit.

God promises that "those who receive the abundance of grace and of the gift of righteousness will reign in life through the One, Jesus Christ" (Romans 5:17).

In a broad sense, righteousness is defined as the state of Him who is as he ought to be, the condition acceptable to God. It includes virtue, purity of life, and rightness, as well as correctness of thinking, feeling, and acting. In other words, righteousness is thinking, feeling, and acting as the person God created us to be.

Think about what this means for you. How does this change your perspective and lighten your load? Make a motivational shift. Our efforts to live a Spirit-filled life are vitally important, but we have to understand we aren't working to be holy and pleasing to God—we already are. We seek God, obey His Word, serve others, and surrender our hearts *because* Christ has made us holy. Without the righteousness of Christ at work in our hearts, we wouldn't care one little bit about holiness.

When you choose holy in the moment, you can rest, knowing that in the righteousness of Christ, who you are is just right and He will help you do what is right.

HOLY MOMENTS FOR RESTORATION OF BODY, SOUL, AND SPIRIT

Rest is the result of trusting God moment by moment. Resting teaches us to live in the freedom of His Spirit, unburdened, full of life, and restored in relationship with God. We experience His rest and restoration as we surrender to God and allow Him to move in the ways He desires. "He restores my soul; He guides me in the paths of righteousness" (Psalm 23:3).

Healing for sin's disease, respite for weariness, mercy for every need—rest is experiencing the restoration of God's work in our lives, making us holy and whole. Rest is knowing our deepest needs are met in Christ: we are loved, forgiven, and accepted. It is finding our adequacy and confidence in Him.

Body, soul, and spirit, we are restored to the person God created us to be, learning to live joyfully. "Christ came to reestablish our identity, showing us what it means to be fully alive as a human—how to live on earth as we were intended to live—a life of complete dependence on the Father," writes Emily Freeman in the book *A Million Little Ways.*[4]

Loving God and enjoying life comes through rest in all we do. As God restores our thinking to the truth, our feelings and behavior begin to change. His *unforced rhythms of grace* teach us to live lightly, holy in the moment (Matthew 11:28 MSG).

We are in the process of learning to live out the Christ-life we have within. In the remainder of this book, we'll explore making godly choices in specific areas of life. Holy living is a choice for every day:

- Rest in faith.
- Depend on Christ's life within you.
- Spiritual transformation comes as you offer your efforts to God and trust Him to complete the work He's begun in you.

My friend, there's hope when you're falling apart at the seams. You aren't alone, and you have a sacred choice releasing the rest of God in your life. The same God who upholds you with His righteous right hand is also the God who holds you up and holds you together. Let your hallelujahs sing, for your soul is set free to rest in life and live in rest as you believe, love, abide, surrender, and rest in God's capable hands.

You do have a responsibility to live righteously, so trust God to work it all together—your effort empowered by His work—making you holy and whole in a way that pleases Him. One thing's for sure, you were *made* to be holy.

And you can rest in that!

SIMPLE REMINDERS TO REST

- The preoccupation of hurry makes it hard to be present with God, self, and others.
- Sabbath is both a day and an attitude to receive the rest of God.
- Jesus can teach you how to live a rest-for-our-souls life free from the burdens of sin, shame, and self.
- Without faith, love, and surrender, the work of trying to make your soul OK is an exhausting, relentless toil of self-effort.
- Righteousness is thinking, feeling, and acting as the person God created you to be.
- Embrace the truth that you are holy and righteous. Sometimes you'll sin, but *sinner* is no longer your identity.
- Knowing you are loved, forgiven, and accepted in Christ sets your soul at ease.
- Holiness is experienced as God restores body, soul, and spirit to the person He created you to be.

PART TWO

EMBRACING TRUTH
IN EVERY MOMENT

Be renewed in the spirit of your mind, and put on the new self,
which in the likeness of God has been created in righteousness
and holiness of the truth. (Ephesians 4:23-24)

CHAPTER 7

MOMENTS TO PRAY

Prayer is simply opening our lives to God, acknowledging our
total dependence on Him. . . . It is an attitude of receptivity in
which we live every moment. It is being open to Him at all times.
It is living in the presence of God, always in the process of being
reshaped and re-created by Him.

—Jennifer Kennedy Dean, *Live a Praying Life*

All afternoon a rainbow keeps watch, and even just a glimpse is enough to
know it's there. Clouds drift, but the rainbow lingers all afternoon, an echo
of an enduring promise. In the rainbow's light, I think of the sovereign care
of God, the power of prayer. This is how I want to live, glimpsing reminders throughout the day of the steady presence of God in a consistent, quiet
rhythm of awareness and activity, prayer, and movement.

How can sacred and secular blend into wholeness, a constant living faith,
reflecting the light of God's grace in our days? Let's ask God to teach us how
to let the activity of our day take on a sacred cadence of prayer that invites
the Holy Spirit to work. Flowing through our hearts, prayer enables us to
receive God's power, His ability *to do, to know,* and *to love* in each situation as
it unfolds.

Prayer transforms any moment from mundane to significant, from tem-
poral to eternal. Through our prayerful lives, God renews our minds and
teaches us to put on the holy and right ways of living in our new selves. Holy
in the moment, prayer changes us and consecrates our lives.

FIRST OF ALL, PRAY

Not every afternoon steps out of time with peaceful relaxation on a beach—times I long for as I sit in traffic, fidgety because I'm running late. What about the kind of days we often have, the everyday normalcy of barely contained chaos?

"I urge, then, first of all, that petitions, prayers, intercession and thanksgiving be made for all people—for kings and all those in authority, that we may live peaceful and quiet lives in all godliness and holiness. This is good, and pleases God our Savior" (1 Timothy 2:1-3 NIV).

First things first, this instruction addresses both time (when) and priority (order). Rather than an if-all-else-fails plan, prayer is our first priority, our first solution, and the thing to do *first of all*. Paul instructs us to pray before we do anything else, the kind of prayer best fitting the situation. Building the habit of prayer makes a difference: we live quiet and peaceful lives in all godliness and holiness.

- When crazy things happen, like when my friend Missy accidently flushed her engagement ring down the toilet...
- When kids track muddy feet across a freshly mopped floor...
- When you muster courage for risky, hard conversations...
- When the boss criticizes and co-workers gossip...
- When the needs of aging parents and active children drain energy as you try to do it all...
- When the phone rings in the still of the night...

In it all.
Through it all.
First of all.
Pray.

PRAY NOW RATHER THAN LATER

"My kids are starting a new school today, and my friend is in the hospital," Adrienne shares in passing. I tell her that I will pray.

"My sister is battling cancer. I'm so worried about her, but I'm also nervous. What if the same gene is running rampant in my body?" my friend Claudia confides over coffee.

"I'll keep you in my prayers," I promise, taking a sip of my drink. Some days, the needs for prayer stack high and heavy on our hearts. We've promised to pray, and we *intend* to pray later when it's quiet. Truth is, it is way too easy to forget to pray when later comes. "Can I pray with you now?" is a more purposeful response than a promise to pray later.

Pray in the moment. Be bold and brave and don't wait until later. Pray now and minister a blessing in the midst of the need. Put your hand on a shoulder, trusting God to give you the words to pray as you let your heart speak. Words that make a spiritual difference as the Holy Spirit helps us to pray (Romans 8:26).

One day at lunch, Lori, a new Christian, made a spontaneous decision to eat at a restaurant she passed. She is excited about learning God's Word, which she calls The Book, and began reading while waiting for her lunch. A woman at a nearby table asked, "I don't mean to bother you, but are you a Christian?"

Telling me the story, Lori said, "I almost freaked out when she asked me, 'Do you know how to pray? Can you pray for me?' I thought, *I don't know how to pray for you. You want me to pray aloud? In a restaurant?* I almost said no; after all, I don't know much about prayer yet. I've never even prayed aloud before."

I asked Lori, "Did you pray? What did you tell her?"

"Of course I prayed. She looked upset, and I couldn't tell her no, even though I felt *really* awkward. When I asked her what she wanted me to pray, she said she was overwhelmed by her first military move and her new husband was deployed. I've moved many times because I served in the Army. I know how she felt! So I prayed, stumbling through a simple prayer, nothing fancy. Afterwards, we talked about moving, and I could tell she felt much better. It felt so good to make a difference."

"Sounds like God gave you a divine appointment so you could pray for this woman. It isn't a coincidence that you have moved many times," I commented.

"Know what's really funny?" Lori asked. "Whenever I read my Bible while I drink my coffee at Starbucks, some stranger comes up to me and asks me to pray for them. It's weird—almost like I've got a sign on my back announcing, 'I pray with strangers,'" Lori laughed. "I guess when I responded to the first woman, God decided to send me more people to pray with. And I hardly know what I'm doing!"

As I listened to my precious friend, I remembered it wasn't long ago when I explained prayer is simply talking to God. At the time she was stunned God would listen to her prayers. Praying in the moment, Lori is experiencing God working through her to encourage hurting people.

There are many simple and quick ways to pray in the moment. Sometimes it may be like Lori's experience, praying aloud with a person. Other ideas include the following:

- Write your prayer on the social media thread or message.
- Send an e-mail or a letter.
- Text a message or make a phone call.
- Ask God's help at the time you face your own need.
- Pray silently for those you meet and situations you observe.
- Say a quick breath prayer such as "Jesus," "Help me, Lord," "I love You, God."
- Pray when God brings a person or situation to mind.

Responsive hearts open channels for God to work through prayer. Holy in the moment, let now-prayer create God connections of strength and encouragement.

HOLINESS LIVES A PRAYING LIFE

Trying to write about prayer, I feel incredibly small, like when you look into an inky black sky blazing with the majesty of the Milky Way. I've started and stopped, written, deleted, and rewritten these words countless times.

Remembering God's power and care frees me from nervous muttering, the default of my soul when I'm not resting in faith.

"How's your prayer time?" Maybe someone's asked you this question, as if prayer is merely an activity rather than a natural part of living in Christ. Maybe you've looked at prayer as something to do, only effective when you can muster up enough faith and form the right words. Drawing solid lines around our definitions of prayer, we squeeze it tight into formulas and techniques and possibly even formal language. We mark set times for prayer ending with *amen*, ready to get on with the rest of our day.

But really, isn't God the "constant gracious listener to our every thought," and doesn't prayer begin "when we bring what we most naturally think about before God"?[1] I'm learning prayer is a way of living that's intimate and organic *as* we abide in Christ. The conversation of prayer is as natural as the thoughts of our minds and the emotions of our hearts.

Dallas Willard cracked open rigid and stale thoughts on prayer: "Don't seek to develop a prayer life—seek a praying life. A 'prayer life' is a segmented time for prayer ... A 'praying life' is a life that is saturated with prayerfulness—you seek to do all that you do with the Lord."[2]

So much more than the asking and the words, prayer expands like an ocean overflowing the heart's borders and joining our hearts with God's.

Prayer is a relationship and yet it's also an activity, action, attitude, and way of living in communion with God. In every moment and for every day—holiness lives a praying life ... rather than a life that prays.

Practicing the presence of God is the key to living a life of unceasing prayer. What wonder to look up at any time of uncertainty or question, any whiff of discomfort, and see the vibrancy of His glory painted across our lives. Living light in the rainbow of faith, prayer makes us aware of God in the present.

Loving God with faith and holiness, prayer is the hinge connecting our experiences with God's grace. "But you, beloved, building yourselves up on your most holy faith, praying in the Holy Spirit, keep yourselves in the love of God, waiting anxiously for the mercy of our Lord Jesus Christ to eternal life" (Jude 20-21). Prayer is the language of loving God that can work into any little moment.

The fact that God is trustworthy, faithful, unchanging, and sovereign yet intimate makes discovering prayer-filled living like waking up to wonder, waking up to holy.

I talked to my sister on the phone recently. "In the Bible it says to 'pray without ceasing,'" she said with a sigh of frustration. "That's impossible—I have a life. I can't just sit around and pray all day. I pray about a lot of things, but how do I pray without stopping?"

Great question—one with an unrealistic answer unless you live a praying life.

To pray without ceasing is to carry on a continuing dialogue with God. Brother Lawrence, a monk who lived long ago, expanded my understanding when I read, "There is not in the world a kind of life more sweet and delightful than that of a continual conversation with God. Those only can comprehend it who practice and experience it."[3]

Continual conversation.

I scribbled these simple words on a yellow sticky note and put it on my refrigerator. For years this 3x3 square of tattered paper reminded me to choose to keep talking to God, to keep seeking Him over and over until intentional choice slowly morphed into habit. Holiness is a continuous conversation always with God, sometimes with others.

Never say amen and keep the conversation going in every little thing as God brings it to mind.

PRAYER IS ACKNOWLEDGING GOD IN ALL OUR WAYS

Thomas Kelly (1893-1941) often wrote about prayerful living. Rather than an alternation between faith and work, Kelly wrote of simultaneity that allows worship to inhabit "every moment, living prayer, the continuous current and background of all moments of life."[4] Something about this statement has stuck with me.

This morning, I'm sitting in my chair, the slightly ratty green one my husband bought at Goodwill when he had shoulder surgery. What was a temporary purchase is still here five years later ... because it's comfortable. It's the kind of chair you can sink into, lean back in, and put your feet up, a chair that wraps its arms around you. In some ways, maybe this chair is a lot like prayer (*not the ratty, green part*).

This is the chair I often sit in when I spend time with God, reading Scripture, jotting notes, and scrawling prayers in my journal. Today I write these verses:

> Trust in the LORD with all your heart
> And do not lean on your own understanding.
> In all your ways acknowledge Him,
> And He will make your paths straight.
>
> (Proverbs 3:5-6)

In this passage I've read many times, God connects truth and prayer with fresh insight. For prayer without trust in God seems closer to wishful thinking or good-luck charms. And many of us have felt this way at times, disconnected and not quite sure if God is really listening.

I remember days, younger in faith, when I wondered if God only heard my prayer if I had confessed all my sins (*and meant it*) and been a very good girl. My concept of God mixed with some sacred version of a cosmic Santa Claus. Fear of punishment by a displeased God made my spiritual life hesitant. Often worried about displeasing God, I tiptoed through life with the self-conscious care of trying not to step on the cracks on the sidewalks of life. Trust was hard to come by when fear buzzed and crackled like static in my prayers.

Trusting God is the foundation of prayer—otherwise why pray? Discover three simple things to develop a praying life.

1. Trust in the Lord. Let me show you what I mean. Be honest, did you buzz past the words *trust in the Lord*? Slow down a moment and consider this:

Have confidence in the Lord with all your heart.

Be secure, without care, in the Lord.

Be bold in the Lord.

And the one that's warm like sun on my skin: *feel safe* in the Lord.

Which one of these meanings of *trust* encourages you today? The fact that God is trustworthy, faithful, unchanging, and sovereign yet intimate makes discovering prayer-filled living like waking up to wonder, waking up to holy.

Whole-hearted trust is a picture of love, isn't it? I've squandered too many moments with half-hearted prayers, as if there's a broken highway of doubt and resistance running right through me. But this verse doesn't say trust God with just part of your heart, and it isn't talking about sort of trusting God.

A divided heart tosses us around on the seas of our questions and troubles, leaving us to wonder if *this time* prayer will work. When it seems God isn't answering our prayers, maybe the issue lies more in our hearts' resistance to believe God is a good Father who doesn't play tricks or give stones instead of bread (Matthew 7:9-11).

Trusting God with all your heart—this is the essence of praying in faith and the foundation of every moment. Prayer flourishes in a relationship of trust built on love, just as faith grows as we learn to trust God with our needs and concerns. The more we love God, the more we trust; the more we trust, the more love grows. Feeling safe and secure, we are freed from doubt and the weight of uncertainty, as we share our thoughts, emotions, concerns, and desires with God.

2. Lean not on your own understanding. This is where prayer gets tricky, bogging down in the muck of what we think we know and insist we want. *Leaning* is a way of praying—to lean on and trust in. To depend on God rather than self is a daily challenge, as our plans and opinions compete for center stage. *Leaning on our own understanding* is the mind-set of the flesh trying to figure it all out, control the outcomes, and get its own bossy-best way.

"I can't believe you did that again. When are you going to learn?. . ." Angry words, harsh with the grit of displeasure, pierce like arrows. I feel attacked and unappreciated. Ready to fight, I whip out excuses and justifications to defend myself. Praying about the situation, I complain to God asking him to fix the person and make them see the how wonderful I really am.

Our own understanding steers crooked with the bias of self.

Wouldn't the better prayer ask for patience and forgiveness? Wouldn't it be healthier to look honestly at the complaint rather than be angry and offended? If I had a dollar for every *my-own-understanding* prayer I've prayed for someone else. . .

Isn't it easy to act like a junior Holy Spirit, knowing exactly what should happen and how it should go? *Lord, make my daughter more organized, help me get this job, and tell my husband to go to church. Oh, and a good parking space would be nice.*

Self-reliance keeps us from depending on God and seeking His answers. Faith is just a word until we trust in the Lord rather than our own perceptions of truth in the moment of our choosing.

---

3. In all your ways acknowledge Him. Your ways include the direction you go, what you do, why you do, and how you live (think, feel, respond, decide).

In every direction, dream, and desire. . .

In every personality trait, preference, tendency, and habit. . .

In every talent, skill, and ability. . .

In every need, every concern, every task. . .

Acknowledge God. Get to know him. Recognize how He works. To acknowledge God is a form of prayer. This passage shows a partnership between God and us. Three instructions are for us, guidance to help us draw closer to God, which results in a promise. Both work together, and yet even in the doing of our part, God provides His Spirit to help us.

GOD'S PROMISE

And He will make your paths straight.

The most important part of prayer is what God does.

Prayer invites God to work in our lives just as they are. By faith we trust, and the Holy Spirit brings it into reality. He is the only One who can straighten our broken and bent ways of living. Friend, let's embrace a praying life, part of God's process of setting our hearts, minds, and wills straight in His right way of doing and being.

Depending on God is the *how* of acknowledging Him, and it is the pathway of prayer leading us all the way with God.

BEYOND ASKING

We often measure the effectiveness and power of our prayer based on getting the answer we wanted. Sometimes we even wait for God to prove Himself by answering our prayers, *or at least I have.* God answers prayers but doesn't take directions. Though a prayer list is a helpful tool, remember prayer isn't a formula or a transaction but an abiding relationship. God faithfully answers prayer, but He's working with a much larger timeframe than the limited ideas we hold in our minds.

Choosing to pray, we respond to God's prompts, and our prayer matures through getting to know God better. We come to understand more of His heart, changing how and when we pray.

Oswald Chambers writes, "the purpose of prayer is to get ahold of God" and is far more about a trusting relationship rather than getting answers.[5] Do you ever find yourself praying as if you are bringing the need to God's attention? (*I do.*) As if He won't know if you don't pray? God already knows, for we have no secrets with Him. Prayer really isn't about convincing God to do what we think needs to be done, building cases, and bargaining for a better deal. Abiding in prayer, we begin to rest in the truth God knows our needs before we ever ask. "It will also come to pass that before they call, I will answer; and while they are still speaking, I will hear" (Isaiah 65:24).

As we keep company with God, He teaches us to reach beyond asking for things. Try asking God to show you the question or the true need He wants you to pray for. And when we don't know what or how to pray, abiding comes in handy for this issue as well: "And the Holy Spirit helps us in our weakness. For example, we don't know what God wants us to pray for. But the Holy Spirit prays for us with groanings that cannot be expressed in words" (Romans 8:26 NLT).

ON YOUR WORST DAYS

Have you ever been tempted to think of Jesus as One who was so spiritual He didn't need to pray? Surely He had a special connection with God, an influence because He was God's son. Right?

Here's what the Bible has to say about that: "In the days of His flesh, He offered up both prayers and supplications with loud crying and tears to the One able to save Him from death, and He was heard because of His piety. Although He was a Son, He learned obedience from the things which He suffered" (Hebrews 5:7-8).

With these words eternity opens, giving us a glimpse of the depth of Christ's heart in prayer. Yielded and poured out, Christ prayed with nothing held back. This passage highlights the humanity of Christ.

Prayer is a reverent offering, especially on our worst days and our deepest heartbreaks.

To *offer* our prayers includes the meaning of presenting a gift or bringing with purpose. *Offering* is the same idea in which friends brought beggars and lame men needing the healing touch of Jesus. They brought the need to the source of help—a visible picture of prayer.

Pray passionately. Pray hard. Pray anywhere and everywhere through the mindfulness of a prayerful life. Jesus prayed on hillsides, in lonely places, in the temple, and in the wilderness of temptation. He prayed in the early stillness of morning, and he prayed throughout many nights. Luke tells us Jesus regularly prayed in the garden of Gethsemane just as He did on the night He was betrayed (Luke 22:39).

When the storms of life crash into your dreams, ask for the commitment to obey, strength to put God's will before your preferences. This lay-it-down kind of prayer releases our hopes and rights, as we surrender our wills to God. Jesus learned obedience through suffering, and sometimes we do as well. Surrender is our hardest, most sacred prayer as, like Jesus, we submit our desires to God.

Christ's obedient sacrifice and our great salvation were ushered in with these soul-saving, sin-breaking, life-raising words: "yet not My will, but Yours be done" (Luke 22:42). When we trust God in our suffering, choosing to pray and accept His will, we release our deepest worship.

On your worst days, pray with a heart stripped bare. The sandpaper of difficulty scrapes off surface layers of success, prosperity, and ability. Remember those nose-in-the-carpet moments? Surrendering my fear to God, I recently prayed:

Lord, I cannot fix myself. I can't change the way I feel right now. I'm overwhelmed, but I realize You don't require me to get it right every time. You don't even ask me to overcome anxiety in my own ability or maturity. You simply want me to be willing to wait for Your provision for my need. To trust You with all my heart in this.

With these honest words, I offered my heart with nothing covered, excused, or justified. In this place of humility, I discovered comfort.

When you can't hold back and when you can barely hold on, pour out your heart in prayer. "Cast all your anxiety on him because he cares for you" (1 Peter 5:7 NIV).

SIMPLE PRAYERS FOR EVERY MOMENT

1. Love: "Abba, I love you. Let me saturate all I do today with love for you."

2. Abiding: "Lord, I want to stay connected to you today. I rely on you, for apart from you I can do nothing" (John 15:5).

3. Appreciation: "Lord, thank You for being patient with me. You are so good."

4. Obedience: "Lord, I'm mad right now, but I'm going to depend on You to handle my anger without sin."

5. Understanding: "Lord what do you want me to know about this?" (Jeremiah 33:3).

6. Praise: "Father, I praise Your holy name."

7. Gratitude: "Thank You for _____" (Philippians 4:6).

8. Offering: "Lord, I love You and I offer this desire to You. I trust You to give what is best" (Romans 12:1-2).

9. Trust: "Lord, I trust You with _____, _____, _____..." (Proverbs 3:5).

10. Wisdom: "Lord, please give me wisdom as we walk together through this situation" (Proverbs 2:6).

11. Work: "Lord, please bless my work. Help me rest in Your presence in the midst of every task" (Colossians 3:23).

12. Comfort: "Lord, You are my Father of mercies and my *God of all comfort*, please comfort me" (2 Corinthians 1:3).

13. Peace: "Lord, You are my peace. By faith, I receive Your peace" (Ephesians 2:14).

14. Worry: "Lord, I bring my worry to You, for I know You care for me. Help me to trust You in this situation" (1 Peter 5:7, John 14:27).

15. Conflict: "Lord, keep me free from judgment, resentment, and bitterness. I pray for [*person I'm in conflict with*]. Show me what I need to know about this situation and help me to forgive freely" (Matthew 5:44, 7:1-2).

16. Sin: "Lord, forgive me for _____."

Holy friend, will you join me in making prayer a priority in life? Let's remind each other to pray first and to pray in this *now-moment* as we let God make all our days a living prayer. As we loosen the grip on our own understanding and seek His truth, we discover holy ground for our souls—the peace of God. "Be anxious for nothing, but in everything by prayer and supplication with thanksgiving let your requests be made known to God. And the peace of God, which surpasses all comprehension, will guard your hearts and your minds in Christ Jesus" (Philippians 4:6-7).

Holy in the moment—we are living in the *amen*. Pray in agreement with the Holy Spirit within you.

Let it be so, Holy Girl.

Let it be so.

SIMPLE REMINDERS TO PRAY

- Prayer enables us to receive God's power, His ability *to do, to know,* and *to love* in each situation as it unfolds.
- First of all pray.
- Pray now rather than later.
- Live a praying life with a continual conversation with God.
- Trust God, acknowledge Him, and don't lean on your own understanding.
- The most important part of prayer is what God does.
- Prayer is a reverent offering, especially on our worst days and our deepest heartbreaks.
- Pray these soul-saving, sin-breaking, life-raising words: "yet not My will, but Yours be done" (Luke 22:42).
- "Cast all your anxiety on him because he cares for you" (1 Peter 5:7 NIV).

CHAPTER 8

MOMENTS TO LISTEN TO GOD

You will never know more about God than the Spirit teaches
you. . . . If He doesn't teach us, we can never know. He is our
illuminator, and if He doesn't turn the light on, we can never see.
He is the healer of our deaf ears, and if He does not touch our
ears, we can never hear.

—A. W. Tozer, *The Mystery of the Holy Spirit*

Something was brewing. I felt God was alerting me, preparing me, and it
wasn't going to be good. " 'What's coming, Lord?' I asked God over and over,"
Salena said as steam swirled above her mug. Around me, snippets of conversations from nearby tables seemed to come to an abrupt halt. I watched her
warm, chocolate brown eyes tell the story before she uttered another word.
She had my full attention.

---

*Attention is a gift empowering us to listen—to others, to God,
and to ourselves.*

Distractions poke and prod, diverting our focus and intentionality. What
good are holy moments if they slip by unnoticed by ears tuned out to the still,
small voice of God who speaks in a variety of ways?

I've known Salena long enough to know she treasures prayer, but I don't
know her hard stories. Leaning forward with both elbows on the table, I sense
God has something to teach me as she shares her story:

I woke with my heart heavy with concern for my husband who hadn't been feeling well over the past few months. Rolling over, I looked at him and said, "You need to go to the doctor. You've got to stop putting this off."

Silently I told God, "You've got to make this stubborn man listen." By 10 that morning, I stood next to my husband in the emergency room. The staff worked with the urgency of something terribly wrong. We didn't have to wait long before the doctors gave a devastating diagnosis.

I'll never forget how the words sounded the toll of a death sentence: acute leukemia. I struggled to breathe as the cold, terrifying words were all too real. Already Sheldon looked more dead than alive as he worsened by the minute. *He's too young. No, God! He's so strong, so healthy,* I wailed in desperate prayer. Within 24 hours, the doctors moved Sheldon to ICU as his organs began to shut down. It all happened so fast. "It doesn't look good. We don't think he's going to make it," the doctor told me with concern and regret. I felt so alone as I prayed. Standing next to Sheldon's bed, I clung to the cold metal of the bed rail like I might fall over if I let go—as if holding onto something tangible could give me strength to face this horrifying illness. As I stood there, God's presence pressed so strong, and He spoke this verse to my thoughts, "I shall not die, but live." (Psalm 118:17 KJV)

Listening to Salena, I wonder, *How do you prepare for something like this?* How do we grow strong in faith that will stand firm when tragedy or trauma strikes? My ordinary morning comes to mind as a stark contrast.

My morning started before my feet hit the floor. Squeezing in time with God, I read Scripture and prayed. I was on a roll until this thought popped into my mind: *I forgot to pay the bills yesterday.*

Knowing the bills should go out today, I stopped to take care of the task. A few minutes later I sat back down. Glancing at the time, I knew the kids would wake any minute, and all hopes of peace and quiet would disappear.

So I tried to pray fast as I tried to sense God speaking through a Scripture passage. Words swam on the page as I struggled to corral thoughts scattering in ten directions at once. *Did everyone get homework done? Did I recharge my phone last night? I have a meeting with a new client today; what am I going to wear? What did I just read?*

DO YOU HAVE SPIRITUAL ADD?

Developing spiritual attention in the scurry of daily life constantly challenges me. You too? Ever feel like you've got spiritual ADD—as in spiritual Attention Deficit Disorder?

With all of our gadgets, social media, technology, and around-the-clock news, we are a distracted generation, and our spiritual lives suffer for it.

When our minds are bulging at the seams, we struggle to notice God's presence in our lives, the many ways His hand is on our days. Reading His Word, our eyes move across the page, but we may struggle to connect with God through the text.

Drawing near to God one moment, but skittering away the next, it's hard to know how God speaks.

The sacred gift of concentration makes it possible for us to get to know God. The ability to look, listen, and learn is a gift to slow and soften our willful hearts with His Word.

Identifying our main distractions is the first step to increasing spiritual attention. What specific things weaken your spiritual focus and intimacy with

God? Loving God and spiritual focus go together. The simple truth is we give our attention to what we value. Ouch, kind of hurts, doesn't it?

"But seek first His kingdom and His righteousness, and all these things will be added to you" (Matthew 6:33).

Talk with God about your greatest frustration with spiritual attention. Ask Him to show you the root issues of your distractions. Think what it would mean for you to deepen your spiritual concentration. Here's the best part: you don't have to do it on your own!

"I will ask the Father, and He will give you another Helper, that He may be with you forever; that is the Spirit of truth, whom the world cannot receive, because it does not see Him or know Him, but you know Him because He abides with you and will be in you" (John 14:16-17).

Learning to attend to God opens a multitude of sacred moments in our everyday lives. Think about the value of spiritual attention shifting our focus from...

- Our plans to God's purposes.
- Our methods to God's ways.
- Our preferences to God's priorities.[1]

Intimacy with God grows as we come to know His heart and cherish His presence.

The simplicity of a regular devotional time for God is a training ground where we listen, learn, and obey God.

Maybe you've wondered if there is a magic formula for hearing God that only the most pious people can discover. As Salena told more of her story, I confess, this crossed my mind: *how did she hear God so clearly?*

God gave me confidence to trust Him, as I had to make life and death decisions with no time to deliberate. I knew things I didn't know—that was the Holy Spirit. I actually knew medical terms I had never heard before, enabling me to share specific things for family and friends to pray. Though I have known God for years, studied the Bible, and learned to recognize His voice, He had never spoken so directly.

Her story reminded me anew that God provides what we need according to His purposes. Knowing how God communicates enables us to recognize Him in the moment. Sharing more of this powerful life experience, Salena continued, "God turned the situation and Sheldon began to improve, making a full recovery!"

"How did you learn to hear God so clearly?" I asked, thrilled to hear of Sheldon's recovery. Thinking for a second before answering, she said, "I think God had been preparing me to face this time for years. God was working long before Sheldon's leukemia to teach me to trust His voice. How many times have you prayed, 'Jesus, I want to know you more?' Lots, right?"

That morning, a table in a coffee shop turned into sacred ground as my friend recounted the years she faithfully studied the Bible and had regular devotional times with God, admitting, "Somehow, I expected to know more of Jesus through dramatic, supernatural, and emotional mountaintop experiences. When my two-year-old son was diagnosed with autism, the doctor said my precious baby would never look me in the eye. Would never speak. Would never be normal. With every word the doctor spoke, my dreams for my son shattered. I didn't know what to do, so I clung to God just trying to hang on. Daily reading of God's Word taught me to listen, and it was in the valley of heartbreak and broken dreams where I came to know Jesus more intimately."

SIMPLE TRUTHS FOR LISTENING TO GOD

When we approach spending time with God as an activity rather than a relationship, we miss the point.

*Hearing God through the Scriptures is about relationship.
The most important thing about having a quiet time is
hearing what God has to say.*

Learning to recognize His voice breaks through the barrier of our misunderstanding and skewed expectations. Here's an example of what can happen as we read for relationship rather than simply for more information.

The Lord God has given Me the tongue of disciples,

That I may know how to sustain the weary one with a word.

He awakens *Me* morning by morning,

He awakens My ear to listen as a disciple.

The Lord God has opened My ear;

And I was not disobedient

Nor did I turn back.

—Isaiah 50:4-5, emphasis added

EXPECT TO HEAR FROM GOD AS YOU READ SCRIPTURE

Hearing God is easier when we come with the faith and expectancy that He will speak to us through His Word. It is tempting to approach having a devotional time with God (quiet time) as one more *good* thing to cram into an overloaded day. Ever catch yourself with the dutiful mentality, "It's supposed to be good for you"?

*We give our attention to God's Word because we are holy,
not to become holy.*

Without the Holy Spirit awakening our attention, we wouldn't care but would roll over continuing our slumber. When we're unresponsive, truth fades into the fog of a sleeping spirit. Meaning is lost in the murmur of countless thoughts muttering in our minds and a lack of concern.

Here are five simple truths about listening to God that we can gather from this passage.

1. Consistency is spiritual discipline. *Morning by morning* echoes the constancy of a daily habit of opening the day by listening to God. Breaking through our distractions, He opens our attention to hear, understand, and respond. I prefer to begin my day in God's Word, but some days it doesn't happen, and that's OK. When my children were babies, naptime worked better. Other seasons, evening was the only time I could manage consistently. The benefit of the morning is that it enables us to keep God's Word on our mind throughout the day, but it isn't a rule. He knows your schedule and your season. Ask Him to show you how to make it work during this season of your life. Friend, please remember this: *Aim for consistency but walk in grace.*

2. Listening begins with God. Isn't it interesting that most of the activity is on God's part? He gives. He awakens. He instructs disciples. He opens. When the Spirit impresses God's Word on your thoughts, it strikes a chord. When a concept or phrase resonates or stands out, the Holy Spirit speaks the Word of God to accomplish God's purpose.

Ask the Spirit to enable you to discern the voice of God. The regular discipline of Bible reading helps us to recognize how God speaks through our thoughts as we read. Instead of drifting in one ear and out the other, truth begins to transform our distracted minds. As God speaks, then reading, listening, and revelation merge like threads woven into a single cord. Our sluggish thoughts perk up with increased understanding and discernment. What we may have glossed over catches our attention as a specific truth, instruction, or detail stands out.

Over time, we notice the difference between God and other voices because of the truth, content, wisdom, and clarity of the thought.

Many times I have wondered, *Lord, was that You or was it me?* The answer is often yes—both. Sometimes we hear God organically, and we may not even realize He is speaking in union with our spirit as it may simply sound like our own thought. But there are also those times we struggle and strain, hoping to hear a specific word and seem to hear nothing. Either way, listening begins with God, and we need to trust Him with the process.

When God speaks, it always agrees with His Word and His character. As we learn more of God through regularly reading and studying the Bible, the more easily we discern His voice. Some of the characteristics of His words include the following:

Love	Joy	Peace
Patience	Goodness	Kindness
Self-control	Gentleness	Wisdom
Righteousness	Contentment	Gratitude
Comfort	Freedom	Guidance
Grace	Conviction	Instruction

3. Listening to God prepares us to bless others. When we listen, we are prepared to encourage the weary. Not just any word. This isn't a pat-your-hand and bless-your-heart kind of word. Who needs that? And it isn't a preachy, I-know-best kind of word. Sometimes the weary one is someone else, but it's often ourselves as well—we all need to hear His life-giving words. God often prompts us to encourage someone, bringing them to mind with a purpose. As He speaks to our attention (putting it on our mind) we are hearing Him.

Earlier today, God brought Cynthia to mind with a nudge to encourage and pray, so I gave her a call. Turns out she was having a hard day and was deeply strengthened by my simple response to God's prompting. The words I had read that morning fit perfectly with her need. God had already prepared me to encourage her.

Has someone ever reached out to you when you needed it most? Few things encourage more than knowing God has prompted someone to minister to our hearts in a tangible way—it's like getting a hug from your daddy!

4. The more we obey, the more we hear God. "I was not disobedient, nor did I turn back." In this passage, hearing means to listen with the intention to obey. When the Spirit speaks God's truth, it has the power to change us—to turn us from rebellion to obedience. As we listen to the truth He speaks and obey, we move forward, trusting God to bring it into our experience. It only takes a step in the right direction to start. As you give God your attention with a desire to listen, trust Him to teach, guide, and empower you.

5. When God speaks through His Word, we are experiencing God. Henry Blackaby writes, "Understanding spiritual truth does not lead you to an encounter with God; it *is* the encounter with God."[2]

For too long, I read the Bible to learn about God, but storing up facts about God didn't change my heart. It was more like arranging knick-knacks to admire from a distance in the living room of my life.

Reading about God can't compare to knowing God by experience as you recognize His voice. Beyond the borders of the pages of the Bible, the Holy Spirit also speaks through our thoughts, intuition, and conversations, as well as through the preaching of His word and the wise counsel of other Christians.

One of the things I love about God is His willingness to communicate with us—often when we most need wisdom, help, or encouragement. Salena's story is a powerful example of the importance of developing a listening heart.

MEDITATING ON SCRIPTURE IS DEEP LISTENING TO GOD

Filling our minds with God's Word, meditation engages deep listening. Letting God's Word seep into our deep places changes our lives when it transforms our hearts and minds. The distance between the head and the heart, between knowing and inhabiting truth, can be a long road, but reflective listening bridges the gap.

Meditating on God's Word blends Bible reading, listening, and abiding together in a sacred conversation with God. *Meditation* simply means "to attend to, to practice, be diligent in, to ponder or imagine." As we ponder the truth, the Spirit opens the Scriptures to our listening hearts.

My friend Sara recently shed new light on meditation when she explained:

> Our goal is to believe and remember who we are as redeemed children of God and then live it! It is the heart that remembers, not the mind. When we only hear with our minds we can't quite grasp the revelation fully and we forget again. But when we hear the voice of love with our hearts, we see and possess the truth we are loved—then we can live loved. How do we hear with our hearts? We first have to know our desperate need (our ache). A daily discipline of listening to God through Scripture gives God an avenue for His love to penetrate and awaken our hearts and our minds. Then we have to choose to believe that God is communicating truth to us.

Holy expectancy brings us to God ready to listen, look, and learn in this very moment. The deep listening of meditation teaches us to read, ponder, and listen with our heart being fully present with God.

As our mind is transformed by God's Word, truth becomes *life* as we choose to live God's way.

In the book *Life with God*, Richard Foster gives this helpful advice:

> The best guard against any handling of Scripture that leaves our souls untouched—and ourselves unchanged—is surrender to the cleansing, forming flow of the Holy Spirit. Simply this means opening our whole selves—mind, body, spirit; thoughts, behavior, will—to the open page before us. We seek far more than familiarity with the text alone; instead we are focusing our attention through and beyond the text to the God whose reality fills its depths.[3]

SIMPLE WAYS TO MEDITATE ON GOD'S WORD

Explore the following ideas to help you meditate on God's Word. Choose one idea to try this week. Some ideas take longer than others, but most can be adjusted to the time you have available.

- Write connections, observations, and insights in a journal. It's helpful to ask, "Lord, what do you want me to know about this?" Take time to listen and write down thoughts, ideas, and verses God brings to your mind.
- Read a verse several times (aloud or silently), emphasizing different words or phrases each time. This simple method helps us slow down and focus.
- Write a verse visually emphasizing words or phrases that stand out to you. Use a variety of style, size, print, script, color, or placement as you listen for words that are especially meaningful. You will often see connections you may not have noticed when you meditate in a visual medium.

- Look up word definitions or read related verses for a deeper understanding.
- Increase your meditation by reading a passage in different translations.
- Meditate through creativity. Draw a picture or mind map expressing your thoughts about a verse. Bible journaling brings meditation, prayer, and art together. Inspirational coloring books also provide a place to process truth in a creative way.
- Get active. Take a walk, praying and talking to God about a specific verse, concept, or passage. Let physical movement enable you to actively reflect on God's Word.
- Make time to pray and meditate as you head outdoors to enjoy nature.

Following the Spirit's lead, meditation may lead you to deeper study or prayer on a specific passage or concept. Journaling is how I most often meditate on God's Word. The meditative process of writing helps me to listen, for my attention wanders with every stray thought. Writing enables me to break through the surface to reach the deeper thoughts by exploring meaning and connection.

You may be groaning, "I hate to write!" (Yes, I can hear you.) That's OK; meditation isn't a one-size-fits-all discipline. There are a variety of sacred pathways you can choose to connect more deeply with God. The important thing is to discover how you are wired to listen to God and meditate on His Word.

Spiritual focus, prayerful listening to God, and meditative Bible reading are practical ways to hear God's voice. As God's presence saturates your life, holiness motivates the choices and responses you make.

As we finished our coffee, Salena concluded, "Day by day, I experienced God's presence, His Word, and His voice through the years of trusting God with my son. God uses everyday faithfulness, in good as well as bad times, to teach us His voice and prepare us for future challenges."

In this special time listening to a friend, Salena reminded me that it's in the everyday that God nourishes our souls. He does amazing things in our lives through daily moments. *The choice to listen is ours.*

SIMPLE REMINDERS TO LISTEN

- The sacred gift of concentration makes it possible for us to get to know God.
- Identifying our main distractions is the first step to increasing spiritual attention.
- Hearing God through the Scriptures is about relationship.
- Expect to Hear from God as you read Scripture.
- Consistency is holy discipline.
- Listening begins with God.
- The more we obey, the more we hear God.
- When God speaks through His Word, we are experiencing God.

CHAPTER 9

MOMENTS TO THINK

No life can be truly changed apart from a change of mind.

—Watchman Nee, *The Normal Christian Life*

"My husband always puts me down," Sandy says. "He thinks he's so smart and smug. I don't know why I even try to tell my side; he never listens. We just keep having the same old argument." As our conversation continues, Sandy lists several past grievances with her husband. Listening to my friend, I'm reminded of how easily our thoughts can keep us entrenched in repeated patterns of conflict and resentment. Both believing they are the one in the right, Sandy and her husband have allowed toxic thinking to weaken their relationship.

Maybe you've experienced a relationship or situation igniting negative thoughts, skyrocketing your blood pressure with strife, resentment, or defensiveness. It's difficult to control your thoughts, settle your emotions, and choose to trust in God in stressful situations. Old messages and beliefs replay in our heads, with thoughts like these:

- *He always lets me down.*
- *I don't deserve this.*
- *He'll never change.*
- *I'll never be enough.*

The difference between holiness and selfishness narrows to a single thought if you act on it. Reacting in the moment, it only takes a split second to let your thoughts run wild or to pay attention to what you're thinking. Consider the distance between a godly choice and a sinful action. Our thoughts play a crucial role in the choices we make, but we live by default when we don't pay attention to our thoughts.

LET GO OF YOUR LIST

Sandy isn't alone in her tendency to keep a mental list of her husband's offenses. Though 1 Corinthians 13:5 (NLT) says love "keeps no record of being wronged," we still face the tendency to keep a variety of records, the kinds we don't like to admit, stored in the recesses of our minds. Though we rarely talk about certain thoughts and beliefs, they can consume a great deal of real estate in our inner thoughts. You won't find this list posted on the refrigerator with a cute magnet. These are the unspoken lists of toxic thoughts corroding our spiritual, emotional, or relational health.

With negative thinking tucked out of sight, we can hold onto those thoughts with an iron grip. Sometimes we keep records against ourselves:

- Situations that didn't work out.
- Reasons we won't succeed.
- Disappointments we've experienced.
- Mistakes we've made.
- Accusations and condemnations we're received.

I'm going to ask you a personal question, and I hope you'll take time to think about your answer. In spite of your accomplishments and talents, do you keep a mental list of all the things you think are wrong with you? The ways you never seem to measure up? The ways someone has hurt you?

Sometimes our list goes the other direction, inflating pride and judgment:

- Reasons why you are better than _____.

- Great things you've done that no one has recognized.
- Behaviors other people need to change.

Squirreled away in the nooks and crannies of our minds are also the lists we keep on other people—ways they have hurt us, let us down, or offended us. When we aren't choosing surrender and forgiveness, it's tempting to keep records of wrongs and lists of complaints while overlooking our own short-comings. This kind of thinking replays the pain, disappointment, or resentment of past issues in the present, distorting how we perceive a current situation. When we do this, no one wins and we take another spin on the merry-go-round of thoughts stuck in the ways of the flesh.

Toxic lists reflect the strategies of living of our old nature, thinking that is chained to self and sin rather than set free in the Spirit. Do you ever experience thoughts that seethe with silent resentment, boil with unrestrained anger, or stifle growth with rampant insecurity? *You're not alone, friend.* None of us is immune to struggling with our thoughts at times. Holy moments are for learning to think differently about our grievances. God has used the simple phrase, *Let go of your list,* to remind me to make better choices with my thoughts.

Just last night at dinner, a frustrating situation made it easy to dredge up thoughts of past arguments. Even as the conversation unfolded, I caught myself whipping out an old, painful list. I prayed, *Lord, I give You my list. Help me to not give in to the temptation to bring past issues into the present. Change the way I am thinking. Tonight I choose patience and forgiveness because I know I can trust You with this situation.*

BE PATIENT; RENEWING YOUR MIND HAPPENS ONE DAY AT A TIME

Your mind is an amazing creation of God—it's one of the ways we reflect His image as we interpret circumstance through our thoughts. In Ephesians 4:17 (NASB), Paul points to the problem that even as believers we can still live (operate) according to the old thought patterns of our flesh when he writes, "So this I say ... that you walk no longer just as the Gentiles also walk, in the futility of their mind."

Unfortunately, we can't flip a switch to turn on a perfectly transformed mind, never reverting to the old ways of thinking. I *really* wish we could—it would be wonderful to never think an anxious or prideful thought. *Ever.* Instead, I'm discovering that God is changing the way I think as I walk through each day abiding, trusting, praying, and listening to Christ. As I'm attentive to my thoughts, God teaches me ways to spot faulty thinking based on lies I have believed.

God is working through our daily choices to embrace truth and reject lies embedded in ideas we believe to be true. Remember when Sandy said, "He never listens?" Our thoughts reflect what we believe to be true in the moment, and emotions, attitudes, and behavior follow our thoughts.

Before we can make different choices, we have to recognize when our thoughts run down the old highways of our flesh. Paul instructed the Ephesians to "Throw off your old sinful nature and your former way of life, which is corrupted by lust and deception. Instead, let the Spirit renew your thoughts and attitudes. Put on your new nature, created to be like God—truly righteous and holy" (Ephesians 4:22-24 NLT).

God works in our minds, and we have to decide to "put on" our new nature. I read this verse for years but never really understood how to "put on my new nature." The truth is you are holy and righteous, and putting on your new nature is learning to live, think and act like who you truly are as Christ expresses His life through you.

THINK ABOUT WHAT YOU'RE THINKING ABOUT

What are the characteristics of your thoughts? Read this list of primary thought patterns and identify your mental habits. Are these thoughts coming from your spirit or from your flesh? Do they help or hinder your life?[1]

Grateful	Defensive	Self-preoccupied
Dissatisfied	Creative	Curious
Hopeful	Passive	Anxious
Courageous	Stubborn	Angry
Determined	Engaged	

Ask God to show you one trait He wants to renew in your thinking patterns as you pray the words of the Psalm 139.

O Lord, you have searched me and known me. . .
you discern my thoughts from afar. . .
Search me, O God, and know my heart!
Try me and know my thoughts!
—Psalm 139:1, 2, 23 ESV

What is one insight or thought you had as you prayed these words? Do you sense God's intimate knowledge of what's going on in your mind? Remember, the Holy Spirit is your Comforter and Helper, so you can trust Him with your real thoughts (like the ones we don't want others to know). He already knows both the *what* and the *why* of your thoughts, but when we pray like this, we invite Him to help us understand ourselves better. We let His light shine in the darkness.

SHUT THE DOOR OF YOUR MIND TO UNWANTED THOUGHTS

Your mind is a door to your soul, and you are the doorkeeper. Though there are many things in this life you can't control, God has gifted you with the ability to open and shut the door to your mind, to choose what you will think about. Let's say a stranger knocks on your door. You're in the middle of something, but you answer anyway. As you open the door the stranger says: "You are worthless. You will never amount to anything. You should quit now before you make a bigger fool of yourself!" How would you respond?

- Tell him to get lost and slam the door?
- Wonder if those were *your* thoughts?
- Stand there, letting him rant on and on?
- Invite him inside to continue the conversation?

This sounds ridiculous, doesn't it? Of course we wouldn't open the door! And yet, the reality of this scenario takes place at the threshold of our minds on a daily basis. Here's the simple truth: You can choose the thoughts you will receive and the ones you will reject. I'm not saying you can keep a thought from knocking at the door—but you can choose whether or not you will agree or dwell on the thought. The more attention and confidence we place on a thought, the stronger it grows. Isn't it time to learn to shut the door to unwanted thoughts?

Sweet, holy friend, you do not have to let your thoughts boss you around, especially when you're relying on the mind of Christ within you (1 Corinthians 2:16). In Christ, you have the power to choose thoughts of . . .

- faith in place of doubt.
- spirit rather than flesh.
- good instead of evil.
- right above wrong.
- purity over immorality.

I'm not saying this is easy, but it is possible because you have a mighty power on your side. Trust the Holy Spirit to help you—He loves to help!

WHAT IS THE SIGNATURE OF THE THOUGHT?

As long as we're on this earth, we're going to need to be intentional with our thoughts. Evaluating the source of our thoughts is a powerful strategy— *who's knocking at your door?*

When we look through the peephole in the door of our thoughts, how do we recognize who's knocking at the door? After all, sometimes bad can look really good, right? One simple way to recognize who's knocking at the door is to consider the character of the thought—who does this sound like? We usually recognize people we know well. When my husband calls on the phone, I know his voice. I can spot my son in a crowd by the way he stands and the way he walks.

The thoughts that come from your flesh have recognizable characteristics you know very well. A few of the characteristics of my flesh include nervousness, people-pleasing, withdrawal, and defensiveness. I've even given my tendency to be anxious a name—*My Inner Wimp*. When one of these thoughts is at the door, chances are it's my flesh. *Hmm . . . that's just My Inner Wimp again.*

The signature of the enemy is deception, and the Bible calls him the father of lies and all that is false (John 8:44). The enemy suggests thoughts to our minds to see if we will open the door and entertain them. When he gets a foot in the door, he can kick up all kinds of strife and angst. For instance, maybe the he-doesn't-appreciate-you thought knocks at the door when your husband doesn't notice something you've done. If you accept the thought, chances are you'll respond to your husband with frustration, anger, or hurt, banging the pots around as you clean up the kitchen. Maybe that's not what he's thinking at all, but you end up relating to him with the thought, *He doesn't care.* In reality, your husband cares deeply about you, but he may be preoccupied with a problem at work. Do you see how easily the enemy can serve up a thought that drives wedges in relationships or creates conflict? The better choice is to shut the door and simply talk with your husband or extend the benefit of the doubt if it isn't really a big deal.

From the earliest days in the Garden, Satan tempted Eve with the lie, "You will be like God, knowing good and evil" (Genesis 3:5). I think it's also helpful to understand that Satan working through the power of sin counterfeits the way God works and contradicts His truth. Satan's goal is to get you to choose doubt, sin, and flesh instead of trusting the nature of Christ in you. The contrast between the deeds of the flesh and the fruit of the Spirit in Galatians 5 shows some of these opposing characteristics.

DEEDS OF THE FLESH

Now the deeds of the flesh are evident, which are: immorality, impurity, sensuality, idolatry, sorcery, enmities, strife, jealousy, outbursts of anger, disputes, dissensions, factions, envying, drunkenness, carousing, and things like these... (Galatians 5:19-21).

FRUIT OF THE SPIRIT

You can also recognize the Spirit when your thoughts express the character of Christ (think fruit of the Spirit). "But the fruit of the Spirit is love, joy, peace, patience, kindness, goodness, faithfulness, gentleness, self-control; against such things there is no law" (Galatians 5:22-23).

Which deeds of the flesh in this passage are direct opposites of the nature of Christ? Use this concept to evaluate the source and signature of your thoughts. List the deeds of the flesh in this passage.

Characteristics of the Spirit Galatians 5:22-23	Deeds of the Flesh Galatians 5:19-21
Love	
Joy	
Peace	
Goodness	
Kindness	
Gentleness	
Self-Control	

Here's another helpful concept: as you evaluate the characteristic of a thought, consider the outcome. Will it lead to grace, peace, and rest? Does it lead to life and love? This is the way the Spirit works. Will this thought stir up strife or agitate negative emotions, reinforce strongholds, or lead to sin?

What is the signature or source of this thought? This is a practical question to identify your thoughts. When the enemy of your soul brings to mind old messages, lies, and negative thoughts, which choice will you make? Will you join the conversation in your mind or slam the door with firm intention? To be intentional with your thoughts in this way is to set your mind. "For the mind set on the flesh is death, but the mind set on the Spirit is life and peace" (Romans 8:6).

Our sacred choice throughout each day is to "walk by the Spirit, and you will not carry out the desire of the flesh" (Galatians 5:16).

TAKE YOUR THOUGHTS CAPTIVE TO CHRIST

I once asked women in a local Bible study to give feedback on a sample of a book I was writing. The next week I went to class interested to hear their responses. As class came to an end, no one mentioned my request. *Maybe they didn't get the e-mail*, I thought. Feeding my courage with a deep breath, I asked, "Did you guys get the sample chapter I sent?" Several women said yes.

And that was all. No comment such as, "I haven't had time to look at it, but I'm looking forward to reading it." The following thoughts immediately came banging on my door:

- My friends don't really care about me.
- I was foolish to ask for feedback—no one wants to read what I write.
- It must have been terrible, and they didn't want to hurt my feelings.

I could let my thoughts run rampant, pull up my old toxic lists, and react with self-pity, resentment, or accusation. At this time, I had a choice to capture my thoughts and bring them to Christ in prayer. Just because these thoughts come to mind doesn't make them true.

In 2 Corinthians 10:5, we find a powerful and practical strategy for making holy choices with our thoughts: "*We are* destroying sophisticated arguments and every exalted *and* proud thing that sets itself up against the [true] knowledge of God, and *we are* taking every thought *and* purpose captive to the obedience of Christ" (2 Corinthians 10:5 AMP, emphasis added).

Do you see the two instructions here? Destroy and take captive. God renews our minds, but part of His process involves action on our part.

Casting down is the act of taking it down with force—we can't be wishy-washy—to cast down is to demolish or refute, to counter the subtle reasoning of opponents. These are strong words because it takes effort and intention to cast down strongholds.

So now what do we do? How do we get rid of these destructive thoughts? We capture our thoughts—recognize and notice them, refuse to let them run wild or build walls. Capturing is more than just recognizing ungodly thoughts; it is bringing them to Christ rather than letting them fester or entrench themselves in our minds.

When we do this, something amazing happens both spiritually and physically. Harnessing negative thought, changing it through awareness, repentance, and forgiveness, and replacing it with truth helps rewire healthy new circuits in our brains, part of God's transforming work in our minds.[2]

Capturing our thoughts calms our minds so we can listen to God. "When we are mindful of catching our thoughts in this way, we change our connection with God from uninvolved and independent to involved and dependent."[3] In other words, we bring God into the negative when we submit our thoughts to Him.

Bring your thoughts into the light of truth and let Christ show you what you need to recognize. "For with You is the fountain of life; In Your light we see light" (Psalm 36:9). Hold fast to what you know to be true and seek to understand your thoughts by the guidance of the Holy Spirit.

PRACTICE *THE HOLY BUT*

In the book *The Rest of the Gospel,* Dan Stone shares an idea that's helped me take my thoughts captive. He calls it *the Holy But,* a simple phrase to remember. On a day when the work is hard and our energy is low we can think, "I know Christ is my strength, but my situation is too taxing." This puts our focus on the problem rather than on the truth. The faith way is to think, "I know my work is taxing, but Christ is my strength." What we really believe comes after the *but.* By faith we reckon God's Word to be fact, we count it to be true. This is the kind of faith God credited to Abraham: "Even so Abraham believed God, and it was reckoned to him as righteousness" (Galatians 3:6).

Perspective can make all the difference when we hold fast to what God says is true.

Which thought pattern is most common for you?

<u>Truth</u> but <u>Problem</u>

<u>Problem</u> but <u>Truth</u>

This may seem overly simple, but *the Holy But* is a practical way to embrace truth in our thoughts. "*the Holy But* moves you from the level of soul, from thoughts and feelings (which are perfectly normal reactions to life's situations), to the level of spirit, to faith, to allowing Christ to respond to situations through you with His life. The situation is the same, but you have shifted on the inside. The Source you are living *from* changes."[4]

Safe in the love of Christ, we can make the choice to release our rights, confront motivations, put aside ungodly thoughts, confess any sins, and surrender our wills. Surrender opens the prison door of the thoughts taking us captive.

Today's rest and freedom comes from yesterday's submission. We replace lies with truth, which changes our perspectives and our experiences as His peace rules our thoughts. With our thoughts and emotions in line with truth, the Holy Spirit continues the process of transforming us into the image of Christ. "And do not be conformed to this world, but be transformed by the renewing of your mind, so that you may prove what the will of God is, that which is good and acceptable and perfect" (Romans 12:2).

It's that important, and it's that practical.

The resentful thought popping into your mind when a friend lets you down . . . recognize your resentment. Catch it. Don't let it fester, adding it to a list you keep in your head. Talk to Jesus, "Lord, why am I feeling resentful?"

If there's a thought that needs dealing with, work it through with Christ: surrender your rights, forgive sins of others, identify your emotions, replace the lies with truth, and receive grace. The angry thought that wants to get back and get even when harsh words hurt . . . catch it. Take it captive to Christ rather than let venom spew from your mouth in retaliation. The *I'm not enough* thought—notice it and say, "Oh there goes that old lie trying to lead me to my flesh. I don't have to let this thought in. Lord, I'm bringing it to You."

SIMPLE WAYS TO THINK HOLY THOUGHTS

Friends, negative thinking isn't going to go away on its own. Those toxic thoughts will not straighten up and decide to play nice. Left unattended, your thoughts will run rampant with complaints, fears, criticisms, envy, bitterness. Take your pick—there's plenty to choose from. When we let the lies of the enemy or the roller coaster of emotions dominate our thoughts, we choose to walk after the flesh, blocking the flow of the Holy Spirit.

Cleaning out mental closets doesn't come easily. Prayerfully consider these strategies to combat negative thinking. Which one can you apply today?

1. Filter your thoughts through the grid of truth: *Is this really true?*
2. Pay attention to recurring negative thoughts enticing you to sin.
3. Identify the signature of the thought: the Spirit, the self, or the enemy.
4. Shut the door to untrue thoughts, reactions of the flesh, and accusations of the enemy.

5. Identify what you really believe in the moment.

6. Memorize key verses and replace lies with truth.

7. Practice using *the Holy But.*

Truth frees you to live in light of the real story of who you are in Christ, to enjoy being you. Bring your thoughts captive to Jesus and trust Him to work the truth into your experiences. Live honestly and bravely by bringing your thoughts to Jesus as He shines truth in your hidden places.

So about that day at my Bible study. When I got no response from my friends, I could have taken my thoughts captive like this: "Lord, I'm taking this too personally. These gals are all busy and tired moms of small children. I know I can trust You. Will You show me what this is really about?"

I *could* have. But I didn't.

I have to confess that on this particular day, I did not take my thoughts captive. This happened in the midst of a long, hard season of discouragement that was part of God's breaking process in my life. It was just one more thing on a long list of problems, and I was emotionally exhausted. Living with my mental door wide open, I allowed these thoughts to join the crowd, and we had a rip-roaring pity party. Every thought on my toxic list showed up! False belief distorted my thoughts as if I were looking in a warped fun-house mirror. We laugh when it's all in fun, but when lies disguise themselves as truths in our thoughts, it's no laughing matter.

In the light of early morning, I brought my thoughts to Christ—better late than never, right? My heart was still floundering as I wrote this prayer in my journal:

Lord, show me how to . . .

- Abide in You as we deal with this together.
- Shut the door of my mind.
- See the true issue from Your perspective.
- Surrender every thought and desire holding me captive.
- *Rest in the truth that sets me free.*

I trust You to guide and direct me as you transform the way I think . . .
One truth
One thought
One holy choice at a time.

SIMPLE REMINDERS TO THINK

- The difference between holiness and selfishness narrows to a single thought if you act on it.
- Be patient; renewing your mind happens one day at a time.
- Think about what you're thinking about.
- Shut the door of your mind to unwanted thoughts.
- Recognize the signature of the thought.
- Take your thoughts captive to Christ.
- Practice *the Holy But*: problem but truth.

CHAPTER 10

MOMENTS TO FEEL

Feeling emotions isn't the problem. Our response to those emotions is what either helps or hinders us.

—Jenni Catron, *The 4 Dimensions of Extraordinary Leadership*

She stands at the edge of the crowd with the hesitancy of one who doesn't belong. With the mind-set of a woman who feels invisible, she prays no one recognizes her. Bent over with pain, she tries to remember the last time she stood up straight.

The last time she ran free or felt healthy and strong.

Time has passed in a blur—the agony of disease and the ache of isolation. She is the woman with the issue of blood, and she's been losing her life for far too long.

Remembering days in the sun, warm with the love of family and friends, she recalls long-ago dreams for the future. But then her body broke to bleed with an unending flow. In time, her soul began to bleed as well, leaking out joy as her emotions whispered daily, *There is no hope.*

She set out to find a cure, discover an answer to the bleeding that took on a life of its own. *Anything to make her feel alive again.* Nothing worked. She has spent all she owns on the fixes of this world and the cures of doctors, but there is no remedy and she has nothing left. Nothing except one desperate hope in the man who is just a crowd away.

She's cried a river of tears as her broken body weakens in the hemorrhage that steals life. This pain keeps coming in a red tide of isolation and rejection worse than the illness. She's forgotten what it is like to feel good. To keep what is precious and hers alone, she's forgotten what it is like to not bleed.

In the noise of the crowd hope flickers, spurring her forward one step at a time. She whispers to herself, "If I can just get a little closer. . . . *If I can just touch the edge of His robe.*"

With every ounce of faith she can muster, she reaches forward, fingers outstretched. Hidden in the anonymity of the crowd, she touches His garment, and in an instant, she's healed. Well. Restored. Without words and without explanations, she knows the bleeding has stopped. She tries to slip away, terrified someone will notice and take back her miracle.

The Miracle Maker asks, "Who is the one who touched Me?" Falling down before Jesus, she declares her healing. And then Jesus speaks words to change her world forever: "Daughter, your faith [your personal trust and confidence in Me] has made you well. Go in peace (untroubled, undisturbed well-being)" (Luke 8:48 AMP).

What troubles the body often troubles the soul, and what distresses the heart often affects the body.

Mind, will, personality, and emotions all connect in sacred territory of the soul.

I've had my times when I'm the woman with the issue, and I'm guessing you have as well.

Mismanaged thoughts, beliefs, and emotions bleed from broken souls. Sometimes they trickle a little at a time, easy to overlook in the roller coasters of life. Other times feelings rush crosscurrent like a riptide in an ocean of troubles.

*Left unattended, stuffed down deep, feelings mixed with
tough times and painful circumstances have a way of
breaking forth from all our efforts to hold them in.*

Maybe these questions have echoed in your heart: Why am I so vulnerable to disapproval? Will I ever overcome my tendency to worry and fret? What's wrong with me?

WHAT ARE YOUR FEELINGS *REALLY* TELLING YOU?

Emotions, a gift from God, are one of the wonderful ways we reflect His image. Feelings add vibrancy and joy to life just as color enlivens a black-and-white photo. However, we don't come into this world knowing how to manage emotions in healthy ways.

Unprepared for the anxiety that invaded during times of transition and insecurity, I didn't know what to do with discouragement and anger I wouldn't allow myself to name.

When we press tally marks against our soul and the shame of our failures cause us to stumble . . . *it's time.* When hidden faults and secret sins fester and drag us down . . . *it's time.* When we've swallowed rejection and believed the lies replaying in our minds . . . *it's time* . . . to embrace truth rather than let feelings dictate what we believe or drive what we decide.

*Thoughts and feelings reveal what we believe in the moment,
and many of those beliefs relate to getting our needs met—
the really important ones like love, acceptance, value, worth,
and security.*

Sandwiched between two strong-willed siblings, I was always the calm one, the peacemaker, and the avoider. Growing up, I felt angry, sad, and lonely at times, but I got over these unpleasant, uncomfortable feelings (or so I thought) and life went on. Though I saw myself as even-keeled, I had no special talent for handling emotions—I had a different temperament, which allowed me to disguise and deny my feelings, often from myself as well as others. I retreated to my room and shut the world away with a book. I grew, but I kept hiding my hard emotions behind locked doors of silence. The feelings too uncomfortable to deal with—speaking up for myself or setting boundaries—I tried to ignore them, hoping they'd go away.

This stuffing method seemed to work for years.

Until it didn't.

My emotions were leaking anxiety, depression, and discouragement despite maturing growth in many areas of life. At times there was a widening disconnect between my emotions and my experience of faith that I didn't understand. *I just needed to try harder,* I told myself, investing more time and effort into family, spiritual growth, profession, and ministry. I'm not saying all these things didn't matter—they are beautiful parts of my life filled with rich blessings and deep faith. There were many successes and happy days; yet, these blessings could not cancel or override feelings and messages that kept me stuck.

Complete, holy, and whole—this is the *amazing* work God is doing in your life. He's already done so many wonderful things in and through you. Working through a life-long process, He also wants to free your heart from the patterns, fears, and strongholds that result when emotions rule your life and lies sabotage your faith. Issues with our thoughts and feelings are often the hardest hours to choose holiness.

One evening I was visiting ministry friends in California. Gathered around the table, lingering over a good meal, my friend said something I won't forget.

> *"You can't grow spiritually beyond where you are*
> *emotionally."*

There is truth to this simple statement explaining many of my struggles. Emotional wounds need to heal in the care of Christ. Little girls hiding in the bedroom become women who conceal their tears, crouching in the closet so no one will hear. They master the art of ignoring pain with a cheerful smile, at least I did. Here's what I never understood in all the battles with anxiety and days of discouragement—hidden wounds fester, and the human heart can store away only so many feelings. I needed to process and release my emotions and misperceptions in the light of love and understanding.

Learning to understand and process our feelings is a crucial aspect of healing, growth, *and* holiness. Anything else is a Band-Aid, protecting the surface but not restoring the heart. As God works to bring mental, emotional, and spiritual growth together, He is making us holy and whole—spirit, soul, and body. The reality is we cannot fully experience holiness when we repeatedly ignore or discount our feelings.

In the book *Emotionally Healthy Spirituality*, Peter Scazzero put words to this struggle I know so well:

> Most Christians do not think they have permission to consider their feelings, to name them, or express them openly. This applies especially to when we reflect on the more "difficult" feelings of fear, sadness, and anger. . . . At the very least, the call of discipleship includes experiencing our feelings, reflecting on our feelings, and then thoughtfully responding to our feelings under the lordship of Jesus.[1]

Though emotional maturity and healing is an often overlooked but crucial component of discipleship, our emotional struggles are part of God's breaking process, part of His timing for coming to the end of our own resources. He never wastes our pain.

Feelings are powerful. Convincing. Enticing. **But they are not truth!**

Emotions can bully and badger, tempting us to believe they carry truth. It all *feels* so real, but feelings are responders and messengers. They hold no power to dictate truth unless we allow them by thinking, "If I feel it, it must be true."

When we allow feelings to convey truth, feelings become beliefs. Here's an example of the progression our feelings can prompt:

- I *feel* rejected.
- I *think* I am rejected.
- I *begin to believe* I am rejected.
- I act like I am rejected.

In reality, feelings just are. I *feel* good, I *feel* mad, happy, sad, hopeful, disappointed . . . and on and on they go.

We need to give ourselves permission to feel what we feel without judging it. Without lecturing it. Without discounting or stuffing it. (I'm pretty good at that one.)

Like blinking lights on a dashboard, negative feelings wave red flags to alert our attention to things God wants to tell us about Himself, circumstances, or ourselves. They signal problems we need to acknowledge and address.[2] Anger, fear, resentment, bitterness, sadness, discouragement, anxiety, and depression are sacred calls for our attention.

- Seek the comfort of Jesus in sad moments.
- Evaluate the messages of resentful moments.
- Search out the root of discouraged moments.
- Choose gratitude in discontented moments.
- Release the hidden expectations of disappointed moments.
- Cry out to Jesus in lonely moments.
- Run to Jesus in outraged moments.

- Remember God's faithfulness in hopeless moments.
- Cling to Christ in dejected moments.
- Release the rights driving impatient moments.
- Reject lies festering in bitter moments.
- Recognize expectations in frustrated moments.

Releasing your rights is to be willing to feel the emotional pain and experience whatever may come during your healing journey. Friend, do you realize surrender *opens* the door to receive God's supply for your needs instead of being controlled by your emotions? Without recognition and surrender, you will keep hanging onto the hurts, demands, and messages that drive negative emotions.

Do you think you could try the sacred habit of attending to your emotions in the care of Christ, seeking the help of a godly mentor or faith-based, biblical counselor if needed? Working with a counselor empowered me to understand the messages in my emotions and thoughts. I'm thankful for the benefit of godly counsel, a deep blessing in my journey. In the light of truth and forgiveness, wounds and fears lose power, and we discover we aren't alone in the struggle. "GOD made my life complete when I placed all the pieces before him. . . . GOD rewrote the text of my life when I opened the book of my heart to his eyes" (Psalm 18:20, 24 MSG).

Circumstances may not change, but submission brings inward growth and peace settling our hearts over time.

HOLINESS ISN'T A RELIGIOUS VERSION OF PERFECTIONISM

In my mind I equated holiness with somehow finding a way to do it all right, especially when I read verses like 1 Peter 1:15-16 (NASB), "but like the Holy One who called you, be holy yourselves also in all *your* behavior; because it is written, 'You shall be holy, for I am holy.'"

Imperfect doesn't mean inadequate, and holiness isn't a religious version of perfectionism. In the realm of our emotions, we sometimes confuse holiness with perfectionism, though we may intellectually know the difference.

Emotions often lead the inquisition to search and inspect ourselves, looking for every flaw and comparing ourselves with others. On some emotional level, I thought of holiness as a kind of cosmic self-improvement plan. We all have particular emotional reactions that trigger flesh patterns or old strategies of living. For me, insecurity and fear have been persistent emotions preventing me from experiencing freedom in Christ at times. I'm guessing you have your own struggles. Are we ready to let go of the standards we have defined for ourselves, as well as the ones others have held over our heads? What if we stop confusing the pressure of perfectionism with righteousness and performance with holiness?

Can you recognize the blur of perfectionism, self-expectation, and self-righteousness in this list of a few of my *if-onlys*?

- If only I got up earlier to pray.
- If only I read my Bible more.
- If only I didn't get so frustrated with my kids.
- If only I were more organized, more prepared, more thoughtful.

If only. I'm not sure what's on your list, but believe me, we've all got our lists of expectations. Sweet friend, don't confuse pressure to perform with God's sanctifying growth process in your new-creation self. I love the way Holley Gerth sheds light on the difference between perfectionism and sanctification—the process of growing in holiness:

Perfectionism is all or nothing.

Growth is little by little.

Perfectionism is all about the goal.

Growth is more about the journey.

Perfectionism is about outward appearances.

Growth is about what happens on the inside.

Perfectionism is about what we do.

Growth is about who we're becoming.[3]

We can't sit around and wait for holiness to bop us on the head. Couch-potato faith isn't holiness. But neither are the standards of the world or the expectations that compel us to prove our worth and adequacy.

When our desire for holiness is motivated by love rather than fear, we exchange the trap of performance for the peace of Christ. When our emotions settle into the unconditional love of God, we pursue Christ free from chains of performance tethering our feet to our flesh.

CHOOSE TO ACT LIKE WHO YOU ARE, NOT HOW YOU FEEL

"I don't feel like a saint—I feel like I'll never measure up to the person God wants me to be. How can I be holy when I struggle with bitterness? Growing up, I had a difficult relationship with my mom, and I still have her critical voice in my head," Amy says as she twirls a blonde lock of hair through her fingers.

We all need frequent reminders that we are a beautiful work in progress: "I am convinced *and* confident of this very thing, that He who has begun a good work in you will [continue to] perfect *and* complete it until the day of Christ Jesus" (Philippians 1:6 AMP, emphasis added).

Do you feel stuck in the old ways of letting feelings define your value and toss your heart around? When feelings overshadow faith, it creates an internal struggle. Amy didn't *feel* holy, but the truth is she is holy and loved in Christ. It's tempting to measure our spiritual condition based on feelings. Maybe you've heard yourself say something like this:

I don't *feel like* God listens to my prayers.

I don't *feel like* God is present.

I don't *feel like God* loves me.

I don't *feel like* I'm saved.

I don't *feel like* I'm forgiven.

I don't *feel like...*

Spiritual growth accelerates as we learn to experience our feelings yet still make the choice to embrace the truth of who we are in Christ. Many have used the train illustration to explain the role of truth, faith, and feelings. If *fact* (truth) is the engine of a train, *faith* is the car following the engine, and *feelings* are the caboose. We struggle every time we allow feelings to take over the engine.

Friend, appropriating truth is far more than head knowledge of knowing the facts—you've already figured that out, right? The more we choose to act like who we are regardless of how we feel, the more our thoughts, emotions, and behavior will align with our true identity as God's precious girls.

You have a choice to act like who you are rather than how you feel. Do you believe this? For instance, I *feel* like I'm playing dress-up as I write this book. But (there's that *Holy But*) the truth is God has entrusted this project to me, and I know He's with me in each word I write. I don't necessarily *feel* His presence, but I count it by faith to be so. I'm choosing to behave like a writer, living out of the talent and ability He's given me and choosing to trust Him with the results.

As for tomorrow, I'll need to make the same choices again.

Are you remembering today isn't the end of your story? Failure isn't forever, and problems will pass as God brings us to completion and full maturity of holiness. Are you speaking truth to your soul that you are worthy of love and acceptance right now? Not *when* or *if*, but in *this* minute.[4] Do you believe this? If not, ask God to enable your feelings to catch up with your faith as you choose to trust Him in the moment.

REMEMBER THE SIMPLE TRUTH OF WHO YOU ARE IN CHRIST

Take time to hold these truths close to your heart. Speak God's truth to your soul every day. Write the truth on note cards and post them where you will see them. By faith, begin to act like these things are true, even if they don't feel true.

There are many days I don't feel holy, accepted, or victorious, but I'm holding on to what is true rather than what I feel.

This lesson began nearly twenty years ago with my first major struggle with anxiety when we moved to California in 2000. Possibly I'm a slow learner, but the reality is the human heart is God's masterpiece, and He works with the canvas for a lifetime. There are no shortcuts to maturing in faith, which is a day-by-day process.

As you make the choice to respond to the truth, your feelings will follow. This takes time, so don't expect it work like extra-strength aspirin immediately relieving your headache. During my days of working with a counselor, I hoped I would feel instant relief from anxiety. With time and practice, I know something in my soul has relaxed as I keep making choices to put truth and faith before my feelings. Again, *the Holy But* has been a helpful way to remember to embrace truth while still acknowledging my feelings.

Practice is the hardest part of transformation, but if we learn to abide with Christ and rest in the truth, we can enjoy the journey. Celebrate the small victories along the way. Use the following list to embrace the truth of who you are in Christ. Let these words remind you to behave like *who you are* rather than *how you feel*. Take time to add to this list as you discover more verses.

IN CHRIST AND BY THE LOVING GRACE OF GOD . . .

1. I am a new creation (2 Corinthians 5:17).
2. I am holy, chosen, and loved (Colossians 3:12).
3. I am sanctified (2 Thessalonians 2:13).
4. I am saved by grace through faith (Ephesians 2:8).
5. I am accepted (Ephesians 1:6).
6. I am forgiven (Ephesians 1:7).
7. I am sealed with the Holy Spirit (Ephesians 1:1).
8. I have the mind of Christ (1 Corinthians 2:16).
9. I am a temple of the Holy Spirit (1 Corinthians 6:19).
10. I am loved with an everlasting love (Jeremiah 31:3).
11. I am God's child (John 1:2).
12. I have new mercies every day (Lamentations 3:22-23).
13. I am free (John 8:36).
14. I have abundant life (John 10:10).
15. I have everything pertaining to life and godliness (2 Peter 1:3).
16. I am filled with the Holy Spirit (Acts 2:4).
17. I am dead to sin (Romans 6:2).
18. I am being transformed by the renewing of my mind (Romans 12:2).
19. I am reconciled to God (2 Corinthians 5:18).
20. I am blessed with every spiritual blessing (Ephesians 1:3).

On your hard days, the ones where feelings try to hijack your faith, remember *the Holy But* and pray like this: "Lord, today I feel rejected, BUT the truth is I am chosen. I feel ashamed, BUT the truth is I am forgiven." Let your feelings be messengers rather than truth-bearers. To fight this battle takes energy, praise, and thankfulness because this is what's needed in the moment.

Pray it, speak it, write it, whisper or shout it—hold onto the wonderful truth and trust God to help you act like the amazing person you are.

SIMPLE QUESTIONS TO PROCESS FEELINGS AND SITUATIONS

1. In this situation, what am I really thinking, feeling, and believing?
2. What need is attached to these thoughts, feelings, or beliefs?
3. What is true?
4. Lord, what is this about? What do you want me to understand about this?
5. What do You want me to know about You, Lord? In what ways am I not trusting You?
6. In what ways do You want to change me, Lord? What attitude or behavior of my flesh am I choosing instead of You?
7. Is there a right I need to surrender? A person I need to forgive?
8. How should I embrace truth in this situation?

THE GREAT EXCHANGE FOR YOUR HEART

The Spirit of the Sovereign LORD is upon me,
for the LORD has anointed me
to bring good news to the poor.
He has sent me to comfort the brokenhearted
and to proclaim that captives will be released
and prisoners will be freed.

. . . .

To all who mourn in Israel,
    he will give a crown of beauty for ashes,
a joyous blessing instead of mourning,
    festive praise instead of despair.

. . . .

Instead of shame and dishonor,
    you will enjoy a double share of honor.
You will possess a double portion of prosperity in your land,
    and everlasting joy will be yours.

—Isaiah 61:1, 3, 7 NLT

Holy moments are for being real with God as we learn to trust Him with the entirety of our lives—every single thing in every circumstance.

Which of these exchanges does your heart need today?

- Good news of hope instead of affliction.
- Bandaging for your broken heart.
- Liberty for emotions, thoughts, or behaviors holding you captive.
- Freedom from lies locking your heart behind prison doors of false belief.
- Comfort for your grief.
- Beauty and significance to replace the ashes of worthlessness.
- Gladness to bring an end to seasons of mourning.
- A double portion instead of shame.
- Joy to chase away humiliation.

Words to encourage your heart and strengthen your soul—this is the intimate ministry of Jesus. What are your feelings telling you? Is there a lie you've believed that has wounded your heart? Are you ready to receive what only Christ can give—healing for a hurting heart? Friend, is this your brave and holy moment to listen to your heart as you bring your feelings into the light of His love?

SIMPLE REMINDERS TO FEEL

- Thoughts and feelings reveal what we believe in the moment.
- God wants to free your heart from the patterns, fears, and strongholds that result when emotions rule your life and lies sabotage your faith.
- You can't grow spiritually beyond where you are emotionally.
- Hidden wounds fester, and the human heart can store away only so many feelings.
- You cannot fully experience holiness if you repeatedly ignore or discount your emotions.
- When we allow feelings to convey truth, feelings become beliefs.
- We need to give ourselves permission to feel.
- Imperfect doesn't mean inadequate, and holiness isn't a religious version of perfectionism.
- Choose to act like who you are rather than how you feel.

CHAPTER 11

MOMENTS TO OBEY

He has called us to be like Himself. Holiness is nothing less than conformity to the character of God.

—Jerry Bridges, *The Pursuit of Holiness*

Does the word *obedience* bring mixed emotions to mind, tempting you to skip this chapter? Do you envision Moses holding the hot-off-the-God-press Commandments written on tablets of stone? Perhaps you think of a long list of *dos* and *don'ts*, secretly wondering if it's OK to watch *Dancing with the Stars* or play cards on family game night. For some, obedience is more about prohibitions than a relationship with Jesus.

Legalism demands keeping rules, but holiness rests in the abundant life of Christ.

In reality, submission starts with a choice motivated by love rather than duty. I'll take love over obligation any day. On my birthday, I don't want my husband to give me a gift because it's his duty. Where's the joy in that? Duty gets lost in the resignation of *have-to*, leaving the heart cold. When my man walks in the door with a beautiful bouquet of roses, I don't want to hear, "Honey I felt like I should give you these roses because it's my duty." That's no way to give a gift.

When motivated by fear or obligation, obeying God feels like a burden rather than a blessing. Without love, obedience can turn into legalism, performing for points or avoiding punishment. *Yes, we've done that.* Love rather than fear powers obedience as Jesus transforms our hearts. When we learn from Christ, we discover God's commands aren't given to weigh us down: "Are you tired? Worn out? Burned out on religion? Come to me. Get away with me and you'll recover your life. I'll show you how to take a real rest. Walk with me and work with me—watch how I do it. Learn the unforced rhythms of grace. I won't lay anything heavy or ill-fitting on you. Keep company with me and you'll learn to live freely and lightly" (Matthew 11:28-30 MSG).

KNOWING + DOING = BLESSING

"For I gave you an example that you also should do as I did to you. . . . If you know these things, you are blessed if you do them" (John 13:15, 17). Knowing and doing are two completely separate states. You cannot DO without the KNOWING, but it is all too easy to KNOW and neglect the DOING.

During the Last Supper, Jesus washes the feet of His disciples, demonstrating the importance of serving one another. *If you know. . . .* this *knowing* is a seeing, experiential thing. *Perceive, notice, discern, discover,* and *pay attention* are a few traits of the word *know.*

Sounds easy, doesn't it? Though it only has two letters, *if* is actually a big word. Here's the problem of *if*—*knowing* and *doing* aren't necessarily givens. The privilege of choice is a crucial part of submission. Following Christ and fulfilling His Word is always a choice. *If* is a word of possibilities and choices, but it's also the gap between the knowing and the blessing, isn't it?

Knowing isn't enough by itself.

You can't *know* yourself into heaven, and you'll never *know* yourself into caring for others. You won't *know* your mouth shut when angry words sear your heart. You don't *know* the truth without opening your Bible. *Knowing* has little comfort as you squirm with remorse when you catch a glimpse of your sins. Left alone, *knowing* is nearly a dead action, having no power to produce life or motivate love.

Knowledge without application runs rampant in today's information-junkie culture. We skim and scan incredible amounts of information, often while juggling several other tasks. (This is usually when I drop something.) We have more Bible study material and more Christian books, talks, videos . . . more information than any other generation in history. Yet how many times have we walked out of church, already overlooking the sermon? Isn't it easy to forget what we've studied in the Bible?

Despite good intentions, my mind is like a colander—information drips out the holes in the gray matter of my overloaded brain. The apostle Paul advised the Philippians, "The things you have learned and received and heard and seen in me, practice these things, and the God of peace will be with you" (Philippians 4:9). Knowing that obedience leads to God's peace, he encouraged them to follow his example.

It's in the doing that the knowing sticks.

SIMPLE WAYS TO DO WHAT YOU KNOW

Ask God to highlight one truth to apply to your life each time you read His Word. Consider how the Spirit can prompt you throughout the day to *do* what you *know*. Here are some simple ideas to apply God's Word in your everyday moments. Has the Spirit ever brought one of these ideas to your mind?

- Ask a question.
- Post a reminder.
- Change an attitude.
- Identify a belief.
- Pray a prayer.
- Write a goal.
- Practice gratitude.

- Share an insight.
- Identify a behavior.
- Let go of an expectation.
- Surrender a right.
- Confess a sin.
- Evaluate a problem.
- Explore an idea.

Knowing AND *doing* reaps the blessing of deeper intimacy with Christ. In this last meal with His disciples, Jesus explained, "Those who accept my commandments and obey them are the ones who love me. And because they love me, my Father will love them. And I will love them and reveal myself to each of them" (John 14:21 NLT). Here, Jesus refers to the quality and intimacy of an active, two-way relationship.

Love is the heart of obedience, and honor is the currency
of love.

How often do we emphasize following commands but neglect the importance of love and relationship? This passage makes it clear we can't do one without the other—*have, keep, and love*—this isn't a multiple-choice question. Henry Blackaby states with blunt simplicity: "If you have an obedience problem, you have a love problem."[1]

As we obey, Jesus makes Himself real to us (John 14:21 AMP). Guiding our hearts as we abide, He instills an increasing desire to live in God's ways.

Abiding in Christ enables us to receive what we need to take the next step. Sometimes we think obedience is all on us, but 2 Peter 1:3-4 clarifies:

By his divine power, God has given us everything we need for living a godly life. We have received all of this by coming to know him, the one who called us to himself by means of his marvelous glory and excellence. And because of his glory and excellence, he has given us great and precious promises. These are the promises that enable you to share his divine nature and escape the world's corruption caused by human desires. (NLT)

In this passage, the Greek word for nature (*physis*) includes the idea of "a mode of feeling and acting which by long habit has become nature."[2]

The more we know the love of Christ, the more we want to obey. Silken strands of grace, holy habits weave together, seamless and interconnected. Does this mean obedience is easy? *I wish.* We all have experiences when following God is a hard choice, but we can't bypass obedience if holiness is our desire.

A deep act of love, surrender happens when we turn from sins, put aside false beliefs, lay down entrenched areas of self, and release expectations. And when we do, resting in faith is the peace that prevails as we trust and obey, depending on Christ as we live by His Spirit. Far more effective than good intentions or religious rituals, these are the daily steps of spiritual growth, the sanctifying work of God in our lives.

Obedience is holiness in action, building a sacred bridge between intention and action as we believe, love, abide, surrender, and rest. Without obedience, holiness is just a lot of nice talk. We want more than that, don't we? Break your big challenges down to small steps by taking it one moment at a time. Trust the Holy Spirit to do in you what you cannot do for yourself. A holy life is making everyday choices to love God and honor His ways.

WHERE THE SPIRITUAL MEETS THE PRACTICAL

Seeking God stirs up changes in our lives. Where thought and feeling meet belief, faith generates action. This is the sacred intersection where the spiritual meets the practical in the midst of an ordinary day.

Let God show you how to put the spiritual and the real-life-live-it-out practical together. Faithful in the little things, the moment-things, this is our daily choosing to love God with . . .

- Each act of love and kindness.
- Each decision to forgive slights and sins of others.
- Each choice to be unoffended when we are left out or let down.
- Each reliance on the power of Christ rather than our own ability.

- Each deep breath of patience when we want to yell and scream.
- Each truth we speak to the accusations of the enemy.
- Each "what if" we counter with "but God."
- Each whisper of His name on our lips.
- Each rejection of pride in our attitudes.
- Each choice to trust God.

God gives us a fresh start each day to walk in the power of the Holy Spirit. Every moment offers a new opportunity to choose God's best. Again, Henry Blackaby helps us understand the power of obedience:

> You come to know God by experience as you obey Him, and He accomplishes His work through you. . . . In many ways, obedience is your moment of truth. What you *do* will . . .
>
> - Reveal what you believe about God;
> - Determine whether you will experience His mighty work in you and through you;
> - Decide whether you will come to know Him more intimately.[3]

How have you experienced God working through a choice to obey? What would it look like to follow God in a situation you currently face?

OBEYING WITH A GOOD ATTITUDE

When we embrace God's ways, one of the by-products of obedience is the blessing of peace. Conversely, when we choose to disregard God's ways, one of the pathologies of sin is discord. Lack of peace, (in whatever form you experience it) provides a warning, calling your attention to a problem. When you know deep in your soul you are on the right track, peace rules. "Let the peace of Christ rule in your hearts" (Colossians 3:15).

Do you ever struggle with your attitude toward obedience? Yes, me too.

Sometimes it is just plain hard to do the right thing. When you struggle with your desire to obey, take time to pray. Thank God for the power of the Holy Spirit who can change your attitude. Ask Him to place His desire in your heart, causing the want-to of your will to become the want-to of obeying. Pray the words of Psalm 51, trusting God to do what you cannot at this time: "Create in me a clean heart, O God, And renew a steadfast spirit within me. . . . And do not take Your Holy Spirit from me. Restore to me the joy of Your salvation and sustain me with a willing spirit" (Psalm 51:10-12).

When our children were little, sometimes they resisted my authority. (Well, a lot, actually). I had fascinating conversations: "Don't hit your sister," "Don't touch the stove," and "Hold Mommy's hand in the parking lot." Years passed and the days of tantrums in the grocery store were long gone, but disobedience took on new forms as they balked at our family rules. As adults, they understand the value of following rules. Believe it or not, they *really* are grateful we didn't let them run wild like some of their friends—the everyone-elses who got to do the things we didn't allow.

Like children, we sometimes respond to God with our arms crossed and a sullen submission in our souls, but this isn't the way of humble obedience. There's a world of difference between *have to, must do, should do,* and *want to.* Toddlers and teens aren't the only ones who resist the rules. It's hard for me as well—and for you too, I'm guessing.

Obedience chafes the heart that's still walking after the flesh. As long as we keep choosing the old reactions and motivations, independence travels a rocky road. Gravel under our tender feet of faith, self-pity, self-reliance, self-condemnation, and a host of other traits of the flesh cause us to stumble on uneven ground. Entrenched sins and strongholds become boulders blocking our way.

Avoiding pain, doing it our own way, or forcing outcomes—these are just a few of the strategies that detour holiness. Instead we experience inner turmoil in a myriad of ways—guilt, remorse, unease, bitterness, resentment, discontent, anger, or fear. Jennifer Kennedy Dean defines sin as "any action or attitude that causes you to miss out on the full glory of God—anything that causes you to be less than you were created to be—God calls 'sin.' He warns you away from sin because He longs for you to know his fullness and your full potential. God hates sin because God loves you."[4]

We all have specific ways we struggle with sin. Reinforced by repetition, these are the signature sins and primary patterns plaguing us. My primary love language is *words of affection*, but the downside of this trait is my tendency to be an approval junkie, working to avoid rejection and disapproval at all costs. This mind-set quickly activates desires to avoid conflict, impress others, and be dishonest about my feelings.[5] When I let this thinking take over, peace is the first blessing to run out the door. Your struggles probably look different from mine, but here's the good news: God helps us choose holiness. "The grace of God . . . teaches us to say 'No' to ungodliness and worldly passions, and to live self-controlled, upright and godly lives in this present age" (Titus 2:11-12 NIV).

May I get personal with you for a minute? What are the patterns and struggles that steal your peace and entice you to sin? Sometimes the sin we are most vulnerable to is subtle, but it's tied to a deep need. What could be the blessing of turning from sin and self in these rocky places in your life? Would you take time to talk with God about your signature sin?

Lord, what do You want to reveal about my sin? What need am I trying to meet when I choose to _____? I release my right to meet my need for _____ in this way. Instead, I will trust You to meet this need in the way You choose. Forgive me for _____. Change my thinking about this temptation. Thank You for Your faithfulness. In Jesus' name, amen.

MOMENTS TO OBEY BRING OPPORTUNITIES TO GROW

Sin isn't always the "big sins" like lying, cheating, stealing, or immorality. Sometimes our sin is just ornery selfishness. This morning I'm making breakfast. Ever on a quest to lose weight, I'm making a nutritional shake. From the office, my husband asks, "Are you making a shake? Will you make me one?" My first thoughts are, *These are my diet shakes. You don't need to lose weight. I don't have many left.* Up pops irritation mixed with selfishness. I know this sounds petty—and it is; that's why I'm telling you about it.

I recognize what's happening.

Noticing my feeling, I silently say to both myself and to the Lord, *Why am I irritated? What's this about? I don't want to think these thoughts.*

With this one little act of attention, I hear the messages of my emotions. When I first discovered the value of recognizing the messages in my feelings, it took a lot of concentration. It was so much easier to wallow in discouragement, fret with worry, or stew in resentment. For a long time, it was only in the big needy emotions like hurt, fear, pain, and self-condemnation that I searched for the messages and surrendered to God. Paying attention to my thoughts was hard because I often didn't like what was lurking beneath the surface as I tried to fix problems that weren't mine to solve.

This morning I realize somehow, in some amazing way, awareness comes more easily now. Maybe not all the time, but I see growth that's the result of faithfulness. With each choice I make to obey, God has been transforming my mind and sanctifying my heart with His truth. When did this mindfulness become a more regular response, a new pattern of thinking?

With fresh eyes, I understand I'm sensing His nudges and hearing His whispers. In the willingness to try, even in my imperfect, inconsistent, shaky efforts, I experience God in a natural and organic way. Over time, a new holy habit has begun to disconnect the old ways of thinking.

Seeing my selfishness is more than enough to turn my heart. *Lord, forgive me for being stingy and selfish. I will gladly make this for my husband. I choose to be thankful he's home this morning.* Even as I pray, God brings to my mind several other small responses of selfishness I've made over the past few days. *Busted.* I didn't even realize a pattern until God brought it to mind. At this point, as God brings it to my awareness, I have another choice to respond so we can deal with it together.

Not so long ago, I would have ignored this reminder to change my attitude and repent of my sins. I'm embarrassed to admit I would have grumbled, "But I deserve this. I'm the one fighting to maintain my weight; he can eat whatever he wants. It's not fair. And by the way, did you see how he got irritated with me last night? That really hurt my feelings." Just so you know, any time you think *I deserve this, it's not fair,* or *but what about him,* your flesh is just getting warmed up.

The most extraordinary possibilities of obedience are multiplied by what God does through our efforts. When we rely on Christ, He opens the door to take the next step, see the next truth, and receive the next blessing. Submission releases the power of God to work the will of God in our frail hearts. A framework for grace, holy moments are for saying yes to God.

Friend, that's not obedience, and it certainly isn't walking in the Spirit. Through the emotions popping to the surface as I get triggered, I'm learning what drives my flesh. I believe it's important to be vulnerable and share our struggles. It's through sharing our stories that we help others break the strongholds, to get to what is behind them, uncovering the false beliefs. And I'm experiencing the helpful truth of these words: "Above all else, guard your heart, for everything you do flows from it" (Proverbs 4:23 NIV). Guarding our hearts is paying attention to our thoughts and emotions because we understand that what we believe, say, and do begins in the heart.

As the blender breaks down the ice cubes, I repent of the hardness of my heart this morning. I ask Jesus to express Himself in me. By faith, I receive His love, patience, kindness, and cheerful giving. And do you know what? I find myself appreciating my husband where just a few minutes ago I was well on my way to a stinky attitude.

It only takes a moment to mix up a smoothie, and it only takes a moment to respond to God—to listen, notice, and respond. To make a difference as we turn from sin.

This isn't an earth-shaking example, but it is a glimpse of faithfulness in the little things, where so much of our lives takes place. As we abide with Christ, the Spirit often works through a thought, a feeling, a prompting, a nudge, a revelation, or a truth. With a still, small voice, He speaks in the small moments—the turn of a page in our Bible, the caress of a child's forehead, a dish in our hands, a conversation on the phone. These are the simple ways holiness grows as we obey in the little things—thoughts, feelings, decisions, conversations, and responses. The Spirit brings something to mind—a truth, an observation, an instruction, a sin, a false belief—and when we're attentive and willing to respond we can choose to . . .

- Practice a better way.
- Confess sin and turn attention to God.
- Trust Him with the results.
- Follow Jesus one choice at a time.
- Make the course correction.
- Replace the false belief with the truth.
- Choose to love.
- Receive grace to do the thing.

Our hearts are so very, very precious and important as God works. How astounding that our eternal God reaches quietly into our days to dwell with us, transforming our wayward hearts. So easily He could crush us with the weight of His glory, the sheer magnitude of His holiness. And yet, He abides with us so gently we often don't feel or perceive His presence. It's in the tiny slivers of time God speaks, renews, forgives, and provides. When we are responsive to God, this is our chance to live fully in the flow of the Holy Spirit. Here and now, embrace the little graces of obedience and choose holy in this moment.

OBEDIENCE LEADS TO JOY

Just as Jesus obeyed the Father, we obey God because we are holy—we don't obey in order to become holy. Because we are living in the Spirit, obedience is part of our new normal as a child of God. It's only when we're walking after the flesh that we choose to sin. When our faith is in Christ, rebellion is no longer the bent of our souls. This is what Paul talked about when He wrote, "be made new in the attitude of your minds; and to put on the new self, created to be like God in true righteousness and holiness" (Ephesians 4:23-24 NIV).

Friend, do you realize our new normal is to delight to do His will, not because we have to but because we want to? Because we love Him. Because that's who we are as new creations. If you're not there yet (none of us is), love God and keep abiding and surrendering as you trust Christ to work in your heart. Obedience enables us to experience the joy of abundant life we were created to live. "If you keep My commandments, you will abide in My love; just as I have kept My Father's commandments and abide in His love. These things I have spoken to you so that My joy may be in you, and *that* your joy may be made full" (John 15:10-11, emphasis added).

SIMPLE WAYS TO OBEY GOD

- Be willing to try.
- Rely on Christ to give you the desire and the will to choose obedience.
- Lay aside the old self and put on the new self.
- Stay connected to Jesus, for apart from Him you can do nothing.
- Release the rights God reveals through your challenges.
- Make daily acts of surrender in the little things.
- Seek to live a praying life, giving God your attention through the day.
- Talk to God in all the little moments.
- Act like who you are rather than how you feel.

- Commit to learning God's Word with a desire to know God better.
- Choose to believe, asking Jesus to help you grow in faith.
- Decide to rest in Christ rather than fret.
- Evaluate your thoughts, feelings, and perceptions through the lens of truth.
- Pray about any thoughts, feelings, or truths God has brought to your attention repeatedly.

Pay attention to trends in your life—repeated concepts in your Bible reading, recurring struggles—these are often where God wants us to change. When you don't know what to do next, keep doing the last thing God told you. Growing in holiness positively impacts your life as you experience Christ's life expressed in your attitudes, relationships, and work.

Want to enjoy your life more? Let's ask God to give us a deep determination for holiness. Remember this simple truth: obedience opens the door to the joy of Jesus. Choose holy in the moment by embracing the truth that sets you free to enjoy your life. Oh yes, holy on, girl. *Holy on!*

SIMPLE REMINDERS TO OBEY

- Knowing + Doing = Blessing.
- Obedience is holiness in action.
- Obedience builds a sacred bridge between intention and action as we believe, love, abide, surrender, and rest.
- Application is where the spiritual meets the practical.
- Obedience chafes the heart that's still walking after the flesh.
- Choices to obey are opportunities to grow.
- Obedience leads to joy.

PART THREE

ENJOYING LIFE FOR YOUR BEST MOMENTS

I came that they may have life, and have *it* abundantly.
—John 10:10b

CHAPTER 12

MOMENTS TO CHOOSE GOOD ATTITUDES

Attitude is a little thing that makes a big difference.

—Anonymous

LIFE IS GOD'S GIFT TO ENJOY

Just take a deep breath. Settle yourself down and relax.

I'd rather throw a book across the room.

Piles of dishes fill the sink, and I forgot to put the wet clothes in the dryer last night. The car won't start, one of the dogs threw up on the carpet, and the sink is leaking. The phone will not stop ringing so I'm just going to unplug it. *Or rip it out of the wall.*

The dogs won't stop yapping, endlessly barking at the man painting the house across the street. Mercy, the man's just getting started. This is going to be one of those days—the kind where nothing goes right—and it's not even 9 a.m. Yes, I *really* want to throw that book.

Attitude is one simple thing to make or break the moment. Life has no shortage of irritations and challenges, that's for sure. Like weeds taking over the yard, complaints multiply when fed by the fertilizer of a negative attitude. Right now I don't feel very spiritual. In fact, I'm one holy mess—and getting messier by the minute if I don't find a way to reset my attitude.

Far more than a doctrine to follow, holiness is a life to enjoy. As God renews our thinking, He teaches us His way of sacramental living. In essence, holiness on the inside changes the way we live, making a true difference in our days. Even the I-want-to-throw-something and the I'd-like-to-wring-your-neck moments.

Enjoying life—the one we're living right now—can be holiness at work. Because we have the life of Christ in our hearts, we have amazing potential, but how often do our attitudes disrupt the moment? That's the question I'm asking myself this morning.

In our journey together, we are discovering the practical power of holiness. Reaching into the nitty-gritty of who we are and how we live, we trust God to bring the reality of our identity in Christ more fully into our experience. Today, I'm proving just how much I need God's transforming work in my life—*especially in my attitude*. I wonder how many blessed minutes I've squandered with a bad attitude?

Learning to make each moment count, we keep choosing to rely on Jesus again and again. And again. Receiving the life of Christ, we are set free from the shackles of bad habits, negative attitudes, misperceptions, and sins that drive us more deeply into a life centered on self rather than the life God has designed for us. Though we have freedom in Christ, we often live like prisoners. Can consecrating the day be as simple as allowing Christ to transform our attitudes?

It's this simple: **Enjoying real life in Christ is experienced through choices we make moment by moment.** We don't always get to pick the moment or choose our situation, but we have freedom to live fully in Christ. When faith rests in the vibrant life of Christ, there is a continual freshness in our lives not dependent on circumstance.

Because we have the life of Christ in our hearts, we have
amazing potential, but how often do our attitudes disrupt
the moment?

The more consistently we abide in Christ, the more fully we can relish each day. Here's a truth to write with big, bold letters where we can see them: "The one who sows to his own flesh will from the flesh reap corruption, but the one who sows to the Spirit will from the Spirit reap eternal life" (Galatians 6:8). I can't help but wonder what I'm sowing with my attitudes.

Sowing scatters seeds of our choices into the day and the lives of the people around us. Carried on the winds of present circumstances, attitudes will harvest something—whether we intended to or not. Have you noticed negative attitudes rarely result in godly thoughts or behavior? Did anything good come from that time you yelled at the kids or vented frustration on a friend? Did slamming the door really help?

When the source of our attitudes is Christ, we will harvest life. In the Bible, the word *life* (*zoe*) is the fulfilling life—the life we often try to gain by our own efforts and accomplishments to feel loved, accepted, valued, worthy, and secure. A gift from God, the noun *zoe* is life "real and genuine, active and vigorous, devoted to God." Blessed, full of vigor, fresh, strong, and endless, *zoe* is the life we are created to live. Enjoying life involves learning "to live eternal life in ordinary time."[1]

Maybe we know this with our heads, but too often we trudge through the week just getting by. We say we're blessed, but we allow inconveniences and minor setbacks to ruin the day. A holy life is one that thrives, not one that's barely surviving. How often have I worn myself out physically and emotionally trying to create a beautiful life rather than receiving an abundant life from Christ? How often have I focused on trying to be godly without relying on the life of God within me?

Are we living as if this Christ-in-me life is on layaway—something we're waiting to experience once we've paid the balance? If we remember the Spirit dwells in us, shouldn't that make a practical difference in our outlook? Oswald Chambers wrote, "We have to receive the revealed truth that He is here. The attitude of receiving and welcoming the Holy Spirit into our lives is to be the continual attitude of a believer. When we receive the Holy Spirit, we are receiving life from our ascended Lord."[2]

HOLINESS HAS EVERYTHING TO DO WITH OUR ATTITUDES

Spanning a wide territory of the soul, attitude encompasses thoughts, emotions, beliefs, perspectives, and inclinations. It also refers to our approaches, mind-sets, moods, points of view, reactions, temperaments, dispositions, and frames of mind. Building blocks of our days, attitudes shape the moment. Affecting what we say and do, attitudes draw us toward God or rivet our attention to self. Our experience of holiness is deeply impacted by attitudes that can be helpful friends or fierce enemies.

Good attitudes are cheerleaders for the soul, open channels through which the Holy Spirit works, bringing God's best into the moment.

Negative attitudes hinder holiness as they trigger flesh rather than encourage faith.

ATTITUDE IS YOUR HOLINESS METER

Have you ever tried to rejoice and worry at the same time? Believe me, I've tried, but worry chases joy away every time. How often have I started the day with a good attitude only to revert to my flesh in split-second reactions of irritation, uncertainty, or displeasure? Does a complaint create happiness? We can't choose envy and love in the same moment, nor can we forgive without releasing bitterness. Just as we can't walk in the Spirit and operate in the flesh simultaneously, godly and negative attitudes pull in opposite directions.

A holiness meter for the heart, attitude reveals whether we are living in grace or floundering in flesh. Gauge the condition of your soul as you reflect on these two questions:

1. Am I becoming more or less discouraged?
2. Am I becoming more or less irritated?[3]

The negative attitudes we most struggle with are likely tied to a combination of circumstances, lies we believe, expectations we hold, as well as our most dominant flesh traits.

Attitudes build bridges among our inner thoughts, feelings, and motivations expressed through our actions. Godly attitudes partner with the Spirit to express the character of Christ in our lives. A signature of the *zoe-life* of Christ, good attitudes are evidence of love, joy, peace, patience, goodness, gentleness, kindness, and self-control (Galatians 5:23). What is the signature of the attitudes you've had lately?

What is the holiness meter of attitude illuminating in your life? Which attitudes are giving you trouble?

The day continues as I struggle to overcome attitudes that reveal impatience as well as a fear of failure. The dogs are still barking, and the man across the street is still painting. Taking time to refresh my heart, I open my Bible and read this verse: "Do everything without grumbling and arguing, so that you may be blameless and pure, children of God who are faultless in a crooked and perverted generation, among whom you shine like stars in the world" (Philippians 2:14-15 HCSB).

Do everything . . . hmm . . . covers it all, doesn't it? I can't think of a single aspect of life that won't squeeze into this *everything* word. Attitude influences our behavior in powerful ways as the condition of thoughts and feelings comes out whether we like it or not.

Comparison, complaint, and criticism are toxic attitudes blocking the flow of the Spirit. A critical outlook can easily create a worn-out habit we hardly notice. But here's the danger of discounting the importance of our attitude: comparison feeds envy, complaint breeds discontent, and criticism ignites pride. Murmuring is discontent on overdrive, and fault-finding is judgment's favorite pastime. Negative attitudes are magnets for the flesh and quickly lead to sin.

Recently, my holiness meter showed me an area where my flesh is inhibiting the flow of the Holy Spirit. One night at dinner, I told my family about my day. I don't recall the situation, but I'll not forget my husband's response. "You sure do complain a lot," he said matter-of-factly.

Immediately I bristled, ready to defend my actions. As soon as I stopped to think, I realized he was right. His words gave me a divine nudge as the Holy Spirit exposed an issue with my attitude. Listening to myself, I recognized how often I mindlessly vent. How about you? Do you find yourself wandering trails of negative attitudes leading to places you don't really want to go?

I pray: "Lord, work in my heart and remove the root of my complaining attitude. Help me to be patient when situations are frustrating. I surrender my 'right' to have all the details of this situation meet my expectations. Jesus, I'm going to rely on You to work on this negative attitude nipping at my heels."

SIMPLE WAYS TO OVERCOME NEGATIVE ATTITUDES

1. Take up humility rather than pride.
2. Mentally prepare for challenging situations with prayer.
3. Add margin in your schedule to reduce the frustration of being late.
4. Stop complaining.
5. Replace the phrase "I have to" with "I get to."
6. Trust God with imperfections and insecurities in yourself and in others.
7. Don't jump to conclusions or assume the worst.
8. Give others the grace you have received from a forgiving God.
9. Treat people the way you want to be treated.
10. Surrender expectations of life to be a certain way.

Friend, I hope you can hear my heart. Choosing good attitudes can be true soul work only accomplished when we rely on the strength of Jesus. Even as I type these words, I fight with my own attitude about a situation at work.

Feeling unappreciated and unfairly criticized, I chafe with an I-don't-deserve-this attitude prickling under the disapproval of a few clients I work hard to serve.

My pride rankles, and the familiar lie that "nobody really likes me" pushes against my choice to rely on Jesus and surrender my right to be thought well of. Do I like it? No, not one bit! The lie of "I'm not very likable" was laid long ago, and it will not die easily. To recognize my thought is to capture it so it doesn't escape my attention. I know if I let the lies win, my attitudes, thoughts, and emotions will trigger the lie that I'm not good enough.

Holy moments are for remembering what's true. Sacred decisions keep in step with the Spirit when it comes to our responses and reactions. In this instance, I remember the message is just an old lie with roots in past experiences of rejection. I know the signature of the enemy who seeks to kill dreams and detour faith. In this *now-moment* I decide I'm not going to play his game today.

NEGATIVE ATTITUDES ALLOW THE ENEMY TO STEAL JOY

At the heart of holiness is the life of Jesus expressed in and through us. Our souls struggle whenever we try to draw meaning and value from the approval of others, the success of our work, or the roles we fill. In John 10:10, Jesus said, "The thief comes only in order to steal and kill and destroy. I came that they may have *and* enjoy life, and have it in abundance [to the full, till it overflows]" (John 10:10 AMP, emphasis added).

Too often I let the enemy rob me blind.

Unwittingly I've allowed him to squash my dreams, stifle my courage, and sabotage my peace. Unchallenged negative attitudes roll out the red carpet, inviting the thief to steal my treasures of joy and peace.

One of my temptations is seeking validation from the approval of others. The flip side of this trait is fear of what people think. Teetering on the edge of the opinions of others, it's hard to enjoy the abundant life of Jesus. An approval junkie, I've searched for joy and peace in the wrong places. Peace is sporadic when you live in a state of low-level anxiety, afraid of rejection. Easily hurt by criticism, fearful of disappointing others, my attitudes hummed with a jittery unease. This causes me to develop an overly sensitive attitude, a source of a lot of insecurity.

Discouragement is another attitude hindering my spiritual growth by allowing the enemy to ransack my emotions. On a frosty January morning I stand in the kitchen pouring a cup of hot coffee. The cold settles in my bones as I peer into the uncertainty of a new year. Swallowing the brew as if it can bring life to my soul, I ask God to help me rest in faith rather than wallow in discontent.

During my quiet time, I write my heart down on a journal page, *Lord, I feel lost in the haze of discouragement. I'm struggling, my kids are struggling, and nothing is going well.* Black ink blurs on the page as the Spirit reveals something true and real about my thoughts, emotions, and attitudes. I have let the enemy steal months—maybe even years—of my life through an anxious attitude.

Living in layers, my heart seeks holiness, but my flesh relies on the old ways of worry, discontent, complaint, envy, and self-pity. In a moment of clarity, I see a vivid picture of the sacred treasure I have allowed the enemy to steal, and I grieve with hot tears.

Until you've looked straight into the cost of negative attitudes, you will keep playing around with the ways of your flesh. As the ink flows, I continue writing, *Lord forgive me. My negative attitudes keep me stuck in discouragement. Will You show me how to live fully here in this gap between yesterday and tomorrow? Teach me contentment even when my prayers seem to go unanswered. Father, release Your holiness in my heavy heart.*

This is the morning a book is born.

These struggles are part of my story of learning to live well in this life of faith. At the time, I don't know this is a breakthrough moment on a continuing journey of healing, wholeness, and holiness as I write, *What is one simple thing I can do today? To learn? To give away? To let go of? If I choose to breathe life-holy into the simple things each day, what will happen? Show me how to choose holiness one day at a time.*

One simple thing—that's all I can handle today. Help me choose holiness in the simple things. Help me find joy. Today I choose life.

One moment at a time.

GRATITUDE AND CONTENTMENT ARE THE FOUNDATIONS OF JOY

Joy and her sister happiness are non-negotiable parts of relishing life. It's important to understand joy is not the absence of pain in circumstances but rather the presence of God in the midst of them. Though we may not have happy or joyful thoughts in every circumstance, these attitudes help us to make the most of the moment. In relation to holiness, joy and happiness play a vital role: "Happiness is *part of* holiness, so that if you tried to describe what it means to be a holy person and left out happiness in God, you couldn't do it.... Happiness in God is the essence of holiness."[4]

My friend Larissa is one of the most vibrant, happy people I know. One day we talked about the importance of contentment and joy—how to find more of it in our actual experiences. She said, "I'm going to practice gratitude every day this month by sharing three things I'm thankful for each day on Facebook."

Counting the goodness of God shifts our perspective away from complaints and problems, the issues and hassles pulling at our attention like magnets. Inspired by this simple decision of my friend, I turn the knob opening the door to joy. Gratitude counters griping, empowering me to see the blessings before my eyes—the ones I've overlooked or forgotten.

A way to simplify the day, gratitude beckons joy by celebrating the little victories I've discounted when I focus on what's wrong rather than what's right.

Five years later Larissa is still posting three grateful things every night. Daily choices to notice the good things have become a good habit, strengthening her faith and literally changing the way she thinks.

What difference can holiness make when we choose good attitudes? The difference is unmistakable as Larissa and her husband, Bill, shine like stars against the darkness of two rounds of cancer with a current terminal diagnosis.

Larissa recently shared how God has blessed her gratitude routine:

As I thought about three things I wanted to list each night, God taught me to focus on what is good. I'm grateful my husband survived his first round with cancer as we have a renewed appreciation for life.

Three-and-a-half years later we were told cancer had returned and spread. An optimistic attitude helps me through the reality of cancer because God has built a strong foundation of gratitude in my daily habits. Some days it's really hard, but God really has protected our hearts through choosing gratitude.

We didn't ask to take this journey, but we sure are going to appreciate the parts we can, encourage the staff and families around us, and give God glory through every step. The power of gratitude is this: we are still enjoying life—with cancer. Making the most of each day we have together, thankfulness gives me the strength to trust God for another day.

Larissa inspires me as I see living proof of godly attitudes opening the possibility of joy in the midst of cancer. She demonstrates a picture of these words: "But godliness actually is a source of great gain when accompanied by contentment [that contentment which comes from a sense of inner confidence based on the sufficiency of God]" (1 Timothy 6:6 AMP).

The Greek word for godliness, *eusebeia*, can also be translated as "holiness." True and lasting contentment is only possible for the heart that has learned to rest in the goodness of God. I appreciate the words of G. K. Chesterton, "I would maintain that thanks are the highest form of thought, and that gratitude is happiness doubled by wonder."[5]

Foundations for joy, gratitude, and contentment build strong walls of protection from the schemes of the enemy who constantly seeks to ravage our souls of every gift of God. "Finally, my brethren, rejoice in the Lord. To write the same things *again* is no trouble to me, and it is a safeguard for you" (Philippians 3:1).

ENJOY LIFE WITH SIMPLE WAYS TO CHOOSE GOOD ATTITUDES

1. Enjoy being you.
2. Love God with a grateful heart.
3. Replace lies with truth.
4. Celebrate little victories.
5. Pray before responding.
6. Trust God in the moment.
7. Smile often—it's good for you!
8. Count your blessings and look for goodness every day.
9. Make time for happiness.
10. Refuse to compare yourself to others.
11. Don't dwell on the past.
12. Spend time with positive people who inspire good attitudes.
13. Learn from your mistakes.
14. Reset negative attitudes by relying on the life of Christ in you.
15. Trust God with imperfections and insecurities in yourself and in others.
16. Start your day in God's Word.
17. Don't allow someone else's bad attitude to steal your happy or ruin your day.
18. Don't assume responsibility for someone else's attitude.

What is one simple thing from this list that you can apply today? Turn your heart toward holiness as you imagine your life without frustration, ingratitude, or worry weighing your heart heavy. Wouldn't you live lightly as the life of Christ flows unhindered by negative attitudes? Release your cares into the capable hands of the God who cares for you, and make this your time to remember you have the *zoe-life* of Christ in you. Holy Girl, don't let joy slip through your fingers! Hold on to hope and receive all you need to make this moment holy with the simple choice of a good attitude.

SIMPLE REMINDERS TO CHOOSE GOOD ATTITUDES

- Life is God's gift to enjoy.
- Good attitudes are cheerleaders for the soul, expressing the Spirit in the moment.
- Negative attitudes hinder holiness as they trigger flesh rather than encourage faith.
- Attitude is your holiness meter.
- Negative attitudes allow the enemy to steal joy.
- Gratitude and contentment are the foundations of joy.

CHAPTER 13

MOMENTS TO LOVE
ONE ANOTHER

Every moment is an opportunity to practice a gesture of love.

—John Ortberg, *The Me I Want to Be*

The Bible tells us we should love one another.

More people should read the Bible. And do what it says, right?

But even when we do, loving one another can still have some messy moments. Our relationships don't always reflect the joyous bliss emblazoned across sunset images on greeting cards. And yet, love is a topic so familiar and so basic we're tempted to roll our eyes and tune out, thinking we've got this down and that the problem is with everyone else. We've heard the admonition that we should love one another so many times it can feel trite. Snore! Zzzz. . . . We jerk awake in surprise when conflict or selfishness erupts in a relationship. We can't escape the truth that loving one another well takes more than good intention.

Your husband is insensitive to your feelings, and the kids won't stop fighting. A friend stirs strife with gossip, and the office has more drama than a soap opera. Aren't these the times you feel like you're *one-anothering* yourself to death, trying to drum up a little love despite the current frustrations? I've had plenty of days when it seems like I am doing all the *one-anothering*. Makes me wonder what has everybody else been doing? Don't they know *one-anothering* is a group effort?

Don't think I haven't told them! Repeatedly.

WHAT IS THE MOST
IMPORTANT THING?

One day, an insincere lawyer, filled with the pride of *I know best,* laid out a trap of a question for Jesus. Used to being the expert, respected as the authority, this man stood up only to look down. On the surface his question *sounded* sincere. "Teacher, what shall I do to inherit eternal life" (Luke 10:25)?

Have we questioned God, inflated with good intentions and suppositions? And how many times have we treated other people this way? Sincere on the surface, but down deep is there another motivation?

We may fool others and we often deceive ourselves, but we cannot fool God. We desperately need His answers to learn how to live the eternal in the midst of our relationships with one another. We can never ask too many times, *What is the most important thing?*

Jesus answered with two simple questions. "What is written in the Law? How does it read to you" (Luke 10:26)? In other words, Jesus prompted the man to think through what Scripture says. "What does it say?" is often the first and best question we can bring to God's words of life. When we think we already know the answers, we inevitably get our priorities out of order, impacting our relationships.

The lawyer replied with the words he'd had memorized since he was young. He'd likely heard them over and over until they became stagnant and lifeless without love. He knew the answers but understood nothing. "You shall love the Lord your God with all your heart, and with all your soul, and with all your strength, and with all your mind; and your neighbor as yourself" (Luke 10:27).

With an unbelieving heart, he recites these words *right into the face of God.*

Just when I am tempted to wag my finger and condemn this man, I roll my eyes and pat myself on the back with confidence, claiming, "Thank God, I don't respond to Jesus like this man." But I can't get the words out of my mouth.

How many times have I reeled off a pat answer with the pride of self-smirking under the surface? It's easy to say, "I love God with all my heart. Sure I love others. . ." but my thoughts are consumed with a thousand other things. I have days when I'm not so different from this insincere lawyer, and I cringe at the thought.

I *want* to be better than that.

Holiness never discounts the importance of loving God wholeheartedly and loving others unselfishly.

But the human heart is often wayward and self-preserving. We all have times of seeking our own needs. Jesus answers insincerity with simple instruction that is the quickest way to eternal life lived in every moment and every relationship.

HOLY MOMENTS ARE FOR LOVING GOD AND LOVING ONE ANOTHER

Revisiting the greatest command, we know Jesus summarized the entire law based on loving relationships. We've looked at this concept from multiple perspectives throughout this book because loving God and enjoying life all come down to the truth that love is the heart of holiness: "This is how much God loved the world: He gave his Son, his one and only Son. And this is why: so that no one need be destroyed; by believing in him, anyone can have a whole and lasting life" (John 3:16 MSG).

God cares about your relationships—how you abide with Him but also how you relate to other people. Do you notice the priority and order of love in the greatest commands? Sacred moments are for loving God and loving one another. God's right order for living is to love God first, then others and self. When we do this, we love from holiness instead of the self-focus of the flesh. Holy harmony with God, others, and self is God's design for life and relationships.

Are you saying to yourself, "I believe this, but why are some of my relationships so difficult? Loving one another shouldn't be complicated, but it is." All we need to do is remember the last argument, critical word, or unkind gesture to know relationships have painful times. It isn't always easy to love others or ourselves. This is the pathology of sin.

Sin inverts and distorts God's design for holy and whole relationships. His commands are not given to be burdensome but to show us how to live, *really live*, the *zoe-life* of God. "For this is the love of God, that we keep His commandments; and His commandments are not burdensome" (1 John 5:3).

Back in the beginning when the world was new, God walked in communion with Adam and Eve. Created to take joy in a relationship with God, the first couple knew God as their Creator and source of life. When temptation slithered into the Garden through the deception tactics of Satan, Adam and Eve made a fateful choice to disobey God, and as a consequence, all mankind upon physical birth into this world has inherited a sin nature separating us from God.

Remember how Satan deceived Eve? "You surely will not die! For God knows that in the day you eat from it your eyes will be opened, and you will be like God, knowing good and evil" (Genesis 3:4-5).

From the first sin, Satan repeatedly attacks humans' relationship with God with the temptation to doubt or disregard God, encouraging us instead to choose to control our own destinies. As a result of sin, this walk-in-the-Garden fellowship with God was broken, bringing death to their spirit, and leaving Adam and Eve no recourse other than to rely on themselves (their flesh and independent living) rather than receive life and identity from God, with God.

"Then the eyes of both of them were opened, and they knew that they were naked; and they sewed fig leaves together and made themselves loin coverings. They heard the sound of the LORD God walking in the garden in the cool of the day, and the man and his wife hid themselves from the presence of the LORD God among the trees of the garden" (Genesis 3:7-8).

In an instant, Adam and Eve saw they were naked as fear and shame created a barrier in their relationship with God, with each other, and with themselves. Their first reaction was to look at themselves. With an inward focus, they saw themselves as exposed and vulnerable, feeling the first hot wash of shame because they were laid bare. Identity, how they knew themselves, shifted to self and the problem of the flesh was born. Reacting to fear and shame, Adam and Eve hid from God and from one another—a cancer of sin infecting relationships. Hiding their nakedness from each other, they covered themselves with whatever they could find, fig leaves. It only took an instant for Adam to blame both God and Eve for the choice he made saying, "The woman whom You gave *to be* with me, she gave me from the tree, and I ate" (Genesis 3:12, emphasis added).

In this passage we see three distinct consequences of sin that still impact relationships today:

1. View of self (identity)—they now look to themselves before looking to God. Finding identity apart from God, flaws and vulnerability need to be covered and protected.

2. Relationship with one another—covering shame, blaming, making excuses, and valuing based on roles rather than identity.

3. Relationship with God—hiding, making excuses, choosing other gods, and casting out of the garden (fellowship with God).

Do you see how sin has inverted God's sacred order from loving God, others, and self to man's system of loving self, others, and then maybe God? Fear and shame rather than harmony and fellowship shape relationships, making it hard to love one another. Remember Jesus said, "The thief comes only to steal and kill and destroy; I came that they may have life, and have *it* abundantly" (John 10:10, emphasis added). Satan attacks life by destroying and stealing from our relationships—with God, others, and self.

OUR GREATEST NEED

Love me is the cry of every beating heart. The question, *Am I loved?* echoes from days in the garden to the one marked today on your calendar. *Am I worth loving?* These are the questions plaguing us in the dark of the night and on the days that ache with loneliness. To be loved, accepted, and valued is a deep God-given need of every human heart. We are created to appreciate relationship with both God and people, and love is the need most satisfying our restless hearts. When our relationships are hurting, it's hard to enjoy our lives.

As I experience my own struggles to love and be loved, I often forget love begins with God. One day the phone rang. "Mom, can you bring me some gas? The car stalled on the way home." Stranded on the side of the road, my daughter watched the traffic whiz past as she waited for me to arrive. "Didn't you know you were low on gas?" I asked, handing her the gas can.

"I knew it was close to empty, but I thought I could wait until after school. I didn't have time to stop before class," she confessed. Gas tanks are simple, but fueling our souls isn't quite so straightforward. We need love just as a car requires gasoline. Pouring time and energy into relationships, service, and work, we give to others in so many ways. If we're running on empty, giving but not receiving, it doesn't take long to find ourselves stranded on detours of disappointment, bitterness, or resentment.

Love one another, even as I have loved you . . .

We love because He first loved us. Before we can love one another, we must begin with these words: "Even as I have loved you" (John 13:34). Love is the key attribute of the nature of Christ who indwells every believer. Have we forgotten this? Have we overlooked the presence of love within, neglecting to receive, abide, and rest in the love of God?

Let's take time to consider God's kind of love. As you reflect on this list from 1 Corinthians 13, appreciate the unconditional love God has for you. This is the even-as-I-have-loved-you of Christ, *agape* love. Only the love of God in us has the power to love others with freedom from sin and self.

Love is patient.

Love is kind.

Love is not jealous.

Love does not brag.

Love is not arrogant.

Love does not act unbecomingly.

Love does not seek its own.

Love is not provoked.

Love does not take into account a wrong suffered.

Love does not rejoice in unrighteousness.

Love rejoices with the truth.

Love bears all things.

Love believes all things.

Love hopes all things.

Love endures all things.

Love never fails.

Truly, unconditional love is a deep expression of holiness.

Quite an amazing list, isn't it? This is the kind of love we long to receive from others, and it's also the kind of love that is impossible to give consistently when we love others from our own resources. *Agape* is only possible when we rely on the Holy Spirit, who enables us to set ourselves aside (our needs and preferences) and love others without expectations.

When love is all about me, agape is impossible.

It is the power of Christ that frees us from the temptation to love in order to get, to love for the sake of self, the what's-in-it-for-me mind-set.

Patience is rarely easy and kindness is simply a good intention when we live with an inward focus. My daughter loved to draw when she was little. With fingers curled around chunky crayons, she drew pictures of houses, flowers, and sunshine. Her favorite thing to draw was the people in our family. She would give each one of us big eyes, wide smiles, and stick-drawn arms. At times, one person was as big as the house, with fingers touching the sun peeking out of the top of the page. Assuming the big person was Daddy, I asked, "Who's this?"

With the candor of a four-year-old, she announced, "Me!"

This is a perfectly natural way to see the world for a child, and every now and then, I revert back to my child-self, loving others as if I'm the sky-reaching, cloud-catching person who fills the whole picture.

Understanding how easy it is to love from self rather than from the nature of Christ within, the apostle Paul instructed the Philippians: "Do nothing from selfishness or empty conceit, but with humility of mind regard one another as more important than yourselves; do not *merely* look out for your own personal interests, but also for the interests of others. Have this attitude in yourselves which was also in Christ Jesus" (Philippians 2:3-5, emphasis added).

Our new identity loves others with patience, kindness, and forgiveness, but we have to unlearn the old tendencies to react with the flesh—impatience, pride, selfishness, and resentment.

Learning to love with the fullness of agape is the unselfing of our souls.

LOVE IS HOW HOLINESS BUILDS RELATIONSHIPS

Reach for holiness and express agape through your thoughts, words, and actions. Choose to love in the nitty-gritty minutes of your day. When your husband forgets to take out the trash, choose patience. Frustrated with the kids? Self-control can harness irritation. When a friend seems to have the perfect family, refuse to be envious. When love is difficult, hold on to hope and keep praying.

Sounds simple, doesn't it?

Simple doesn't always equal easy.

Choose to receive this agape-love of Christ and let it flow out to those around you in the choices you make. Abiding and resting in Christ enables you to make the most of your life by sharing what you've been given.

Filling up with God's love energizes the words you say and how you spend your time. What will happen when you take it one moment at a time, depending on Jesus to empower you to give your very best self in loving others? How will your relationships be different?

Holy moments will change the way you love.

WHAT HAPPENS WHEN GOD ABIDES IN US?

Sprinkled throughout the New Testament, many *one-another* verses add living color to God's desire for holy relationships. Looking at the many *one-another* verses, we discover God's best ways to reflect His nature in our world. "Beloved, if God so loved us, we also ought to love one another. No one has seen God at any time; if we love one another, God abides in us, and His love is perfected in us" (1 John 4:11-12).

What can happen when we set aside our petty differences, the things that don't matter but divide? Forgiving one another is one of the love-one-another ways God matures and completes (perfects) us. Power ignites when we give what we have received—the needed blessing of acceptance that is healing to the soul—*accept* one another. When we overcome selfishness to *serve* one another, we demonstrate the love of God to a world that doesn't know God. When we love others, we demonstrate what the love of God looks like. Take time to look up and meditate on these one-another verses. Each of these verses shows us how to choose holiness by loving one another each day.

CHOOSE TO LOVE IN MOMENTS TO . . .

1. Confess and pray with one another (James 5:16).
2. Be at peace with one another (Mark 9:50).
3. Be devoted and give preference to one another (Romans 12:10).
4. Be of the same mind with one another (Romans 12:16).
5. Build up one another (Romans 14:19).
6. Accept one another (Romans 15:7).
7. Admonish one another (Romans 15:14).
8. Care for one another (1 Corinthians 12:25).
9. Serve one another (Galatians 5:13).
10. Bear one another's burdens (Galatians 6:2).
11. Choose tolerance, gentleness, and patience with one another (Ephesians 4:2).
12. Speak truth to one another (Ephesians 4:25).
13. Be kind, tenderhearted, and forgiving with one another (Ephesians 4:3).
14. Regard others as more important (Philippians 2:3).
15. Bear with and forgive complaints against others (Colossians 3:13).
16. Comfort one another (1 Thessalonians 4:18).
17. Encourage and esteem one another (1 Thessalonians 5:11-14).
18. Do what is good for one another (1 Thessalonians 5).

19. Motivate, encourage, and assemble with one another (Hebrews 10:24-25).

20. Choose fervent love covering a multitude of sins (1 Peter 4:8).

21. Be hospitable to one another (1 Peter 4:9).

MOMENTS TO ENCOURAGE ONE ANOTHER

"So speak encouraging words to one another. Build up hope so you'll all be together in this, no one left out, no one left behind. I know you're already doing this; just keep on doing it" (1 Thessalonians 5:11 MSG).

"I know you are struggling to make it through this," Michelle said during the days thyroid disease left me anxiety-ridden and sleepless for months. "You may not have faith right now, but I believe you're going to get better. I am standing in the gap and praying for you. I'll check in with you every week," she continued. Michelle's encouragement made a difference in my life at a time I had little bravery; she came alongside with her courage, helping me to stand firm in faith. The sacred gifts of her love, time, and faith not only made a difference at the time but also nurtured a friendship spanning twenty-five years. God has given me opportunities to return the gift of encouragement, prayer, and support as Michelle has battled her own health problems.

Encouragement today plants seeds for tomorrow as God works through love.

MOMENTS TO MOTIVATE ONE ANOTHER

"Let us think of ways to motivate one another to acts of love and good works" (Hebrews 10:24 NLT).

We sit in the sun and a breeze blows gently as we visit. I am having lunch with Brenda, a gifted writer and speaker I've worked with a few times. Leaning forward, Brenda looks me in the eye and says, "Ginger, you should start writing seriously." I laugh because this seems an unlikely possibility, intimidating and far beyond my ability. With eyes of love, Brenda saw something in me that I couldn't see. Putting a name on it, she called an unrecognized gift to the surface, motivating me to let God do something new in my life. At the time, I didn't know it, but this simple conversation became a directional moment in my life.

A few weeks later God gave me my first idea for a book. When the idea came, I recognized it because Brenda had spoken a word to stir something in my soul. When we take time to encourage others, building them up in ways that make a difference, God can do far more than we imagine in the moment. Ten years later, Brenda and I are colleagues in a ministry that wasn't even a dream at the time of that conversation. You just never know what God will do when we take time to motivate and encourage another.

MOMENTS TO FORGIVE ONE ANOTHER

A commitment to love can strengthen you to say to your soul, "Unforgiveness is not an option." When we walk in the daily grace of surrender and forgiveness, the Holy Spirit moves in powerful ways.

When a parent has let you down...

When your husband dismisses your concerns...

When your child forgets your birthday...

When your co-worker blames you for something...

When a friend betrays a confidence...

When ...

Make the sacred choice to forgive.

By this love.

They will know.

We are His disciples.

SIMPLE WAYS TO LOVE ONE ANOTHER

Not only for the bigger events but also for the everyday moments, love is a gift of grace. When we abide in Christ, love becomes a lifestyle, a habitual way of relating to others. "Little children, let us stop just *saying* we love people; let us *really* love them, and *show it* by our *actions*" (1 John 3:18 TLB).

Show appreciation.

Listen with a smile.

Be present.

See those around you.

Share laughter with friends.

Respond with a blessing.

Greet a stranger.

Be patient in line.

Let someone else go first.

Notice the little things.

Celebrate success of others.

Choose kind words.

Offer to babysit.

Meet a need.

Share lessons learned.

Show how to do something.

Comfort with a thoughtful gesture.

Appreciate good effort and hard work.

Do things together.

Say thank you.

Value the contributions of others.

Forgive. Every time.

Don't we love it when other people do these things for us? I can hear you thinking, *I'd love to do these things, but I can't keep up with my life as it is. How do I find time?*

God will give many opportunities in the midst of your day to encourage others. So as you go, love one another in practical ways fitting the moment. Love in one simple way at a time.

*Small daily acts of intentionality turn bad days around,
and as we express the love of Christ, loving one another is a
powerful way God turns lives around.*

Don't miss the moment, for when we listen to Jesus, living out of our true identity in Christ, holy hearts say yes to loving one another.

SIMPLE REMINDERS TO LOVE ONE ANOTHER

- Don't dismiss the importance of loving God whole-heartedly and loving others unselfishly.
- God cares about your relationships.
- Sin inverts and distorts God's design for holy and whole relationships.
- Satan attacks life by trying to destroy our relationships—with God, others, and self.
- Christ frees us from the temptation to love in order to get.
- Love is how holiness builds relationships.
- Depend on Jesus to empower you to give your very best self in loving others.
- Encouragement today plants seeds for tomorrow as God works through love.
- You never know what God will do when we take time to motivate and encourage one another.
- The Holy Spirit moves in powerful ways through daily acts of love and forgiveness.
- When we abide in Christ, love becomes a lifestyle, a habitual way of relating to others.

CHAPTER 14

MOMENTS TO BLESS
YOUR CHILDREN

Maternal love is a miraculous substance that God multiplies as
He divides it.

—Victor Hugo

I sit on my bed, knotting up the hospital-blue sheets with fidgety hands. When
I checked into the hospital a few days ago, I was just me. Now I am a mom. As
we fill out the discharge papers, it's time to leave the hospital with our baby in
a car seat I'm not quite sure how to work.

What if I can't do this? I have no idea how to be a parent. What if I break him?

My emotions swing from joy to terror and back to wonder. And then
back to a fear that makes me slightly dizzy. My room is across the hall from
the nursery, and I've already learned to distinguish my son's cry from all the
other babies. Part of this might be motherly instinct, but mostly it's due to the
fact he has cried nearly nonstop in the 24 hours since his birth. The prenatal
classes my husband and I attended taught us how to change a diaper and give
a bath, but somehow this just isn't enough preparation to bring a baby home
from the hospital. Especially one crying all night and half the day. I've only
been a mom for a day and already I'm lost. Even the professionals can't quiet
his cries.

Over the years, the desire to be a good parent will often spiral into the
self-reliant pressure of *Super-Mom Syndrome.* I wanted to be the best mom

possible, honoring God with faithfulness, which in my mind meant a lack of dysfunction and conflict—getting it all right. It meant raising children who love Jesus and mature into successful adults. Somehow I felt responsible for my children's happiness. (I found out later that meant I was co-dependent, but that's another story.) I'm being very honest here, so don't mess with me; we all have some version of a picture-perfect desire of what family life should look like.

The first few years, I ascribed to the *from-scratch* method of parenting. We used cloth diapers, and I made our own baby food. I learned to bake whole-grain bread, read Bible stories, started my kids on chores, read books on discipline, and considered homeschooling my children. Again, all good things when pursued with faith firmly planted in Christ rather than self-effort. I would have made my own Kleenex if I had thought of it. Just kidding!—sort of.

Super-Mom Syndrome thrives on doing all the right things to build the perfect family. Despite the hard work of parenting, the idea and the reality of life with children don't always match. Time passed quickly, and before I knew it, we had three wonderful children. (Just so you know, cloth diapers stopped with the second child, and by the third child, I was just relieved to get them all fed.) When you have more children than hands, a certain level of chaos is a daily part of life, no matter how brilliant your parenting strategies.

Fear of failure and desire for perfection in any forms are merciless taskmasters triggering the flesh into hyper-drive in the name of godly parenting. We fix, cajole, control, and contrive, often unaware of what we're doing. When *Super-Mom* flesh shows up, parenting can seem more like a project than a privilege on some days. The flesh treats being a godly mom as a job to achieve and a role to prove, rather than a gift and ministry to receive the life of Christ in the context of family. Oddly enough, all this *great* parenting may look wonderful on the outside, but there are days when mom is hanging on by a thread that could snap at any minute.

Despite good intentions and effective discipline plans, we discover our precious babies have wills of their own. Doing "the right things" (however you define that) doesn't equal perfectly behaved children or ensure peace in the family. In reality, the details of family life include messy moments where holiness can seem to be out of the picture.

Again, it's a quick step from trusting God to the pressure-cooker of working harder to find the right strategy, solve all the problems, clean the house, discipline the children, oversee the homework, make homemade cupcakes for the class party, and pick up the soccer player—all before dinner. Mom, if this is you, just stop and take a few minutes to breathe before you keel over!

Pursuing excellence as a parent is a mighty hill to climb, but how we get to the top makes all the difference.

Good intentions can quickly default to our own efforts when we are not walking in the Spirit in a moment-by-moment abiding relationship with Jesus.

Holiness impacts families as God transforms our minds, growing us in faith as we discover the beauty of grace. Loving God and choosing faith is not disconnected from daily life. Instead it is the fuel, divine energy to help, convict, comfort, and instruct. When we learn to live in the overflow of the Spirit, setting aside the tendencies, fears, and phobias of our flesh, Jesus works in our hearts from the inside out as *Super-Mom* begins an internal transformation into *Saint-Mom*.

As I began to understand the cost of perfectionism (for me the cost was usually anxiety and fear), the pressure to perform relaxed with grace. This has been a layered journey of God working on deeper levels through the years. I learned to let go of my self-effort to create the perfect family.

Parenting involves so much more than making meals, giving baths, doing homework, correcting behavior, and saving for college. Godly parenting is built on the foundation of loving God, for it is His sanctifying work in our hearts that empowers us to love our children free from the needs and dictates of the flesh.

Each day we have many opportunities to bless our children. Sacred choices are often disguised in the mundane minutes of kind words, kissing boo-boos, applauding cartwheels, correcting misbehavior, choosing patience, and teaching truth, to name a few.

Learning to rely on Christ has made a difference in my parenting—not just for my children but also for me. From the reality of bringing our first baby home from the hospital to taking the last child to college, fear has been a deep part of my story. As I look back on the years, I recognize many times I parented out of fear.

- Fear of what if.
- Fear of doing it wrong.
- Fear of conflict.
- Fear of messing my kids up.
- Fear for health and safety.
- Fear they wouldn't make friends.
- Fear we'd make wrong decisions.
- Fear they weren't happy.

You name it, and I worried about it. And then some, for good measure.

Fear drives some of us to respond inwardly, while others struggle with outward reactions of anger. Uncomfortable with conflict regarding discipline, I often placated, compromised, or withdrew, while my husband, when operating in his flesh, tended to go the other direction. When crossed, he was more likely to respond with angry words, sarcastic retorts, or strict decrees. I tell you this simply to illustrate the truth that our responses may differ according to our flesh patterns, but it is all the same root issue of parenting from our brokenness rather than from the righteousness of Christ's life.

SIMPLE TRUTHS TO PRACTICE HOLINESS IN YOUR PARENTING

Make the most of each day, as you love your children in the countless ways best coming from you, that special woman called Mom. Your love and wisdom bless your children at every age. Each and every day look for the extraordinary in the small joys and little miracles filling your life. After twenty-five years as a mom, these truths still guide my choices and encourage my heart.

1. Parenting is a sacred journey rather than a destination or accomplishment. Parenting isn't just for raising children—it is also for growing up parents. God uses our struggles in parenting to mature our faith. If you're a parent, raising children is a vital part of God's work to bring you to the end of your self (self-effort) and to teach you to trust Him. (If you aren't a mom, God will find another avenue—you're not off the hook.)

The situations we can't handle, the problems with no simple solutions, the conflicts and confusion—these challenges train us to acknowledge God rather than lean on our own understanding. We have the choice to take each day as it comes as we abide in Christ. Parenting is a very effective training ground for walking in the Spirit rather than striving in the flesh.

2. You don't have to do this alone. You don't have to be an expert to begin the parenting journey, and you don't have to be *Super-Mom*. Just in case you missed that one, I'll say it again: *You. Do. Not. Have. To. Be. Super-Mom.*

In Christ, you are stronger than you know (Philippians 4:13). And as you grow in holiness, you will discover the value of godly habits and Spirit-led choices to influence your parenting.

Holiness in your heart will become holiness in your parenting, as Jesus will help you continue to choose holy in the moment.

---

3. Start with your own heart. One of my struggles as a parent was over-giving at the altar of what I perceived to be good parenting but under-valuing the condition of my heart. Life with children is demanding, and it takes purposeful effort to attend to your soul, cultivating faith and love for God. For me, learning to evaluate the messages in my thoughts and emotions is a level of soul care easy to neglect in the frazzled days of life with children.

As you grow in holiness, God teaches you how to abide, surrender, and rest in a moment-by-moment dependence on Christ. Sister, keep turning your heart toward God, receiving the life of Christ.

4. Recognize when you parent with the traits of your flesh. Trusting God rather than relying on self is an intentional choice. Holiness includes freedom from the hurts of the past and the old ways we've learned to handle life.

- "In order for my children to be OK, I must _____."
- "In order for me to feel OK, my children must_____."
- "Life will be better when my kids _____."

How we fill in the blanks to these statements can help us recognize when we are placing confidence in the flesh rather than abiding in the Spirit.

Prayerfully consider the following questions, asking God to reveal areas for surrender and growth:

- Do your expectations line up with God's priorities?
- Are there areas you are trying to do God's job with your children? How's that working?
- Are you parenting by grace or by rules? By faith or by feelings?
- What impact is fear or anger making in your family?
- Are you addressing only the externals rather than nurturing the heart?

Remember that surrender doesn't mean it is unimportant or wrong to want good things, but when desires become *must-haves* or demands, we will pursue them in the flesh by manipulating, controlling, fixing, fretting, or grumbling. These actions do not create sacred moments and rarely bless our children.

SIMPLE WAYS TO BLESS YOUR CHILDREN

The day he did push-ups in the middle of the four-lane road, I thought my teenager had lost his mind. A group of lanky, long-limbed teenage boys, full of life and bravado, waited for the bus, egging each other on to greater feats of foolishness. At times it seemed some alien life form inhabited the once-congenial, cute child of days gone by. Then there were the days of increasing conflict and emotional outbursts from our daughter. Where did our sweet-natured child we used to call "Sunshine" go? *Why has everything suddenly become a battle?*

Sitting at the kitchen table in the quiet of the morning, I bow my head to pray. Heart tender and tired, ready for truth to encourage, I open my Bible and read: "But if we look forward to something we don't yet have, we must wait patiently and confidently. And the Holy Spirit helps us in our weakness. For example, we don't know what God wants us to pray for. But the Holy Spirit prays for us with groanings that cannot be expressed in words" (Romans 8:25-26 NLT).

Today isn't the end of the story. God settles my heart, reminding me parenting involves waiting with patience and confidence for what hasn't happened yet. Holy in the moment, I rejoice that today isn't the end of the story but simply one day of a wonderful journey that is passing quickly.

Pray every day. The Spirit helps us in our weakness, praying alongside us with the perfect will of God, even when we have no idea what to pray. Pray for your children, for your parenting, and your marriage daily. In the moment I pray, "Lord, I need Your patience and perseverance today. I rely on You to give me wisdom and help me pray for our family. Bring to mind what I need to pray for my children today."

Wait on God with patience. God strengthened me with a deeper understanding of patience—not just to keep it together as a mom but also to wait patiently for Him to work in my kids. Patience for self-control and patience for faith—we need it both ways.

Some days and phases seem to inch along. Your baby will sleep through the night. The days of tantrums and squabbling will pass. Eye-rolling teens will appreciate you eventually. Be willing to wait and let nurture, time, and wisdom do their jobs. Some days may seem long, but the years are short.

Teach your children to love God and live by His Word. No one can teach your children the blessing of following God like you can. Keep His words in your heart and in your conversation. Embracing truth and loving God with your life will profoundly impact the development of their hearts. You may not see this at the time, but trust that God's Word never returns empty.

Don't neglect discipline and training. You are the parent; it's your job to say no when needed and to enforce wise rules (Hebrews 12:11). Teach your children manners, respect, responsibility, and kindness through your words and examples (Ephesians 4:32). Discipline isn't only correcting behavior but is also training the heart.

Enjoy your kids every day. You will never have this day, this age again. Find something to appreciate, smile, laugh, or relish daily. A joyful heart creates energy and gives perspective. Your kids are amazing, and so are you. Rejoice in the special qualities of your children and marvel at the wonder of God at work in your lives.

Don't let the hard days cloud joy and appreciation of the gifts you have. Build the habit of seeking joy each day.

Set the atmosphere in your home. Don't let nagging, complaining, or whining become the norm in your family. Negative attitudes are contagious and can become bad habits. With a slow creep, they invade your days if you aren't keeping watch. Both kids and adults can struggle with these unpleasant behaviors.

Be careful with your words. Never forget that encouraging words empower our children (Philippians 2:14). Make the good choice to speak life and truth to your children. Kindness matters, for words can wound deeply.

Let no unwholesome word proceed from your mouth, but only such *a word* as is good for edification according to the need *of the moment*, so that it will give grace to those who hear. Do not grieve the Holy Spirit of God, by whom you were sealed for the day of redemption. Let all bitterness and wrath and anger and clamor and slander be put away from you, along with all malice. Be kind to one another, tender-hearted, forgiving each other, just as God in Christ also has forgiven you. (Ephesians 4:29-32, emphasis added)

Laugh often and let yourself play. Make the most of your days and delight in the little blessings along the way. Enjoy spontaneous and planned fun with kids of every age. It's easy to get bogged down with chores, work, attitudes, and stress. Find joy in the small, ordinary moments with laughter and play (Proverbs 17:22).

God is greater than your mistakes as a parent. We've all made many mistakes as parents. A goal that seemed like such a great idea at first backfires. You struggle with frustration and impatience, sometimes yelling or saying things you wish you hadn't. Truly, there are days with children pushing you past your limits, frazzling your very last nerve. *The struggle is real.* Mom, if you are struggling beyond what you think is healthy or what you can handle, reach out to someone. Enlist the support of a godly mentor, good friend, or Christian counselor. All three of these kinds of support have been valuable in my life. And yet in it all, through it all, God is faithful. As we seek holiness, God enables us to grow through our struggles.

HOLY MOMENTS TO RELEASE YOUR CHILDREN

Holy in the moment, we are exchanging *Super-Mom* for *Saint-Mom*. Kiss perfectionism goodbye as you rely on the One who makes you holy, perfect, and complete by putting soul, body, and spirit together. Pray, sow seeds of faith, implant the word of God in your children, and be a godly example as you nurture faith and saturate their lives with the prayers of *Saint-Mom*.

The morning my twenty-one-year-old daughter was set to leave for

Australia, I woke with a heavy heart. A one-way ticket and the reality of saying goodbye pressed hard against the joyful knowledge that she is following God's lead to work with YWAM (Youth with a Mission) for the next few years. I wanted to whine, "Why a country so far away? Isn't there someplace closer You could send her?" I want to complain, "Two years seems like forever." I started to worry, but I caught my thoughts, turning them to praise for God's faithfulness in raising our children. Mostly, I felt tender and small, sad about saying goodbye.

I was up early before the last-minute scurry to leave the house. God spoke to my heart through His Word and the impressions I wrote on the page of my journal. "Be still and be in this moment. Know that I am your God—your helper and strength. I am your source and your blessing. Open your hands— to let go as well as to receive. It's time to release, and this is good."

I opened my heart to what God is doing in my life and in my family. I asked for strength and faith to entrust my grown child into His hands with joy rather than sadness. I will keep trusting and resting. I will open my hands to hold onto God rather than cling to what I cannot keep, my children and the way things were when they were younger. In a way, this is hoarding the past, and today is a time for something new. *Something holy.*

I will try not to hold onto the past in an attempt to ensure happiness and security for the future, for I cannot store yesterday's grace and blessings to bank for tomorrow. The very thoughts in my head are evidence of the work God has done in my heart. Holiness is an open hand, trusting that God is sufficient for each day and every need. I open my mind to receive grace for a new season—grace to let my children go in faith.

All too soon, cars and taxis crowd the departure lane in the chill of the early morning. Rushed, we say our goodbyes, and my heart wants to cling when I think it is likely to be a year before I hug her again. There's a part of me that cannot even take it in, and I force myself to breathe.

Chest tight and watery eyes leaking love, I whisper in her ear, my face pressed against her silky hair, "I'm so proud of you. I love you so much." A car horn honks. Words cannot express what is inside—the wonder, excitement, joy, fear, love, and loss all tied up together in a tangle of emotions and faith. I hug her tight and let go. Though the distance weighs heavily, the possibilities and faithfulness of God empower me to loosen my grip. I have this tangible sense of releasing her into God's great care as she steps out into the wide adventure of her own calling and faith.

Holy in this moment, there is no better place to be.
She is ready. Ready to fly. Ready to go.
And so am I.

SIMPLE REMINDERS TO BLESS YOUR CHILDREN

- *Super-Mom Syndrome* thrives on doing all the right things to build the perfect family.
- Fear of failure and desire for perfection in any form can send the flesh into hyper-drive in the name of godly parenting.
- Pursuing excellence as a parent is vitally important, but *how* we get there makes all the difference.
- Good intentions can quickly default to our own efforts when we are not walking in the Spirit.
- Sacred moments are often disguised in the mundane happenings.
- Learn to recognize when you are parenting with the traits of your flesh.
- Make the most of each day as you love your children, because no one else can be their mom.
- Parenting is a sacred journey rather than a destination or accomplishment.
- Teach your children to love God and live by His Word.
- Discipline isn't only correcting behavior but is also training the heart.
- Through every parenting challenge, God is faithful. Today is not the end of the story.

CHAPTER 15

MOMENTS TO BE A GOOD FRIEND

It seems they had always been, and would always be, friends.
Time could change much but not that.

—A. A. Milne

Longing for friendship and connection starts early in life.

Every girl knows there's no age limit on friendship. My daughter toddles out to the pool with her baby-doll stroller, clomping in her grandma's pretty red shoes. She loves the clackity-clack of hard soles on hot cement. Grandma follows close to make sure this little one stays away from the edge of the pool.

Cute as a bluebird, she perches on the side of the pool in her ruffled bathing suit. Greeting everyone in sight, she chirps, "Hi. What's your name?" By the end of the afternoon, she has met many of the adults and most of the children at the pool. With her three-year-old wisdom, no one needs to tell her this truth: there's just something special about a friend. A gift from God, friendship is an important part of enjoying life.

BE THE FRIEND YOU WANT TO HAVE

Over the years, God has richly blessed me with growth, encouragement, and inspiration through friendships with other women, something I love to call *the gift of girlfriend.* Side by side and heart to heart, authentic friends add joy and fun to our lives, but they can also help us grow through life's challenges. Relational beings, women need to connect with trusted friends. More and more, I'm learning to ask God to help me be the friend I want to have, choosing to trust Him with the results. When I focus on blessing and encouraging others, it's easier to let go of the need to impress or compete.

ARE YOU WELL DRESSED
FOR FRIENDSHIP?

Little girls love to dress up. When my daughter was four, a pink tutu was her favorite outfit for everything—dancing in ballet class, playing in the yard, or running errands with mom. And what better outfit to wear to a play date with friends?

We might be too grown up to wear a pink tutu, but we never outgrow the joy of friendship. It doesn't matter whether a girl is 5, 15, or 50, friendship is an important part of life.

Say yes to the dress! Here's what good friends wear:

So, as those who have been chosen of God, holy and beloved, PUT ON a heart of compassion, kindness, humility, gentleness and patience; bearing with one another, and forgiving each other, whoever has a complaint against anyone; just as the Lord forgave you, so also should you. Beyond all these things put on love, which is the perfect bond of unity. Let the peace of Christ rule in your hearts, to which indeed you were called in one body; and be thankful. (Colossians 3:12-15, emphasis added)

Always the right attire for every relationship, godly character traits will never go out of style. To *put on* means to consider it so. You have all you need to live this way and to share it with others. Enhancing our relationships, sacred moments are grounded in the love of God. As we live in the fullness of our identity in Christ, the insecurity of our souls is transformed into confidence, affirming we are chosen, holy, and beloved by God. Getting dressed (receiving, appropriating, and reckoning) in the Spirit's qualities comes down to choosing to rely on what God has given us—His ability to be compassionate, kind, humble, and gentle.

We can give because we've received.

We can love because we've been loved.

We can forgive because we've been forgiven.

When we put on the qualities of the Spirit, we are free to enjoy our friendships with open hearts.

Confident and secure in Christ, we don't need to draw love and acceptance from others. It's great when we have that—but it isn't a demand or expectation anymore. Resting in Christ unravels threads of anxiety and pressure weaving through friendships when we feel insecure. Can I tell you how much this frees me to be OK if everyone doesn't like me? I may not like it, but I know we aren't going to bond with everyone. Receiving the fullness of God's Spirit, our needs for love, acceptance, worth, security, and value are met. We can focus on giving to others, friends and family, trusting God to meet our needs, which He often does through people in our lives. He has a way of working it all together for good.

Make the simple choice to put on God's qualities as you get dressed each day. Let the practical action of putting on your clothes remind you to prayerfully put on the Spirit. Just as you wouldn't go to work without your shoes, don't leave the house without abiding in the love of God.

As you think about the Colossians verses above, note the qualities demonstrating the nature of Jesus. Is there an attribute of the Spirit missing from your relational wardrobe? Do you have a relationship in need of a few intentional choices like these?

EVERY FRIENDSHIP BEGINS WITH AN INVITATION

She walks into the unfamiliar, crowded room with a sense of dread. The boisterous noise of hundreds of students laughing and talking over lunch makes her long to be anyplace but here. Will anyone notice the new girl and invite her to join their table? Looking into a sea of unfamiliar faces, she wants to fold in on herself. Be invisible.

Months later, the newness has worn off and my girl has made a few friends, but transitioning into a new school takes time. One afternoon, she bursts through the front door with a perk in her voice I haven't heard in way too long. There's a bounce in her step and a sparkle in her eye that I've missed. "Friends invited me to the game tonight," she says.

It feels good to be invited, doesn't it? An invitation can make a big impact. A gesture of inclusion, an invite can warm our hearts, making us feel wanted and accepted. We never truly outgrow some level of this desire to know we are included (at least I haven't). Do you recall how important invitations were when you were growing up? Life's greatest joys and trials often revolved around being invited or excluded. *Remember?* We've grown up now, but inside we still want to belong. Many women still battle loneliness and long for connections deeper than the latest post on social media.

Every great friendship begins with an invitation. Yet too often we find ourselves hanging back, waiting for others to reach out and take the first step. I believe it's time to bring back the neglected grace of invitation. How many of us hope for others to invite us, yet we neglect to invite as well? When everyone is waiting for someone else to do the inviting, we're all busy but not connected.

How can we overcome some of the barriers to the joy of friendship? Perhaps it starts with this one simple thing: don't wait to be invited.

THE MINISTRY OF INVITATION TO INVEST IN RELATIONSHIPS

Inviting friends to do things is important. Invitations can be easy to overlook in the midst of schedules overloaded to the breaking point. There are no shortages of barriers to building meaningful friendships. We forget how powerful an invitation can be to initiate, develop, and deepen friendships.

Commitments and responsibilities sometimes make me feel guilty for taking time to have fun with friends. Maybe you've felt this way too. Here's what I say to that—it's time to stop feeling like we're shirking our *real* duties by spending time with friends. Seriously, stop it! Remember all those *one-another* commands? How can we encourage, help, love, and pray for one another if we don't know anyone? The body of Christ would be incomplete without investing in godly friendships. If this is your struggle as well, let go of the productivity myth and give yourself permission to have fun with friends. Ask God to show you a healthy and practical balance for your season of life. Pick up the phone and invite a friend to do something fun.

Another barrier to building good friendships is busyness and lack of planning. Do you forget to invite others because of a full schedule, tempting you to ration energy as if it is a nonrenewable resource? Some days I just run out of steam. But really, my biggest challenge is simply remembering to plan ahead. Sometimes I just get into a rut of running the same routines, overlooking the importance of making plans before the last minute. I'm queen of the spontaneous invite because of the bad habit of not thinking ahead. This is something I'm working on—sometimes I remember, and other times I get washed away by the latest wave of things crowding time for friendship.

When I neglect to plan, I miss *in-person* time with friends—longing for close connections. Some days I'm hungry for the togetherness of friendship, for I've starved myself of the deeper relationships by snacking on posted photos and updated statuses that give the illusion of meaningful connection in a busy life. This can be a very real challenge, especially for moms with young children and those with jobs of solitary work. Don't we all long for those precious moments of listening and being listened to in honest conversations?

Inviting friends *over* creates many memorable moments. The pressure of entertaining can also prevent us from inviting friends to our homes. When we think of invitation as an opportunity to minister to others, we can relax and put the importance on spending time with people. The house doesn't have to be spotless, and the meal doesn't have to be five courses on your best china. Truthfully, I wouldn't even know how to prepare five courses, and I'm feeling good if the table is cleared off when friends arrive. As for the countertops? Forget it! I will never win the battle of the kitchen counter. If you love to decorate and your cooking can compete with Rachael Ray's, then enjoy being you; just let me know what time to show up. Either way, the important thing is to invite others *over*, extending the gift of fellowship and hospitality.

Inviting others *in* is powerful. And really, isn't invitation a ministry? God moves in powerful ways through the encouragement of friends. Doesn't it feel good when we can let go of insecurities and put the importance on investing in relationships? Inviting others goes far beyond going to parties or coming over for coffee. Holy moments for friendship happen when we invite others *in*. The best invitations are the ones in which we open our hearts to deeper connections and faithful friendships. Authenticity, transparency, and genuine interest are sacred choices for godly friendships. These are the invitations that open hearts and cement friendships. These are the invitations that can change lives.

Think of how friends have impacted your life. As I think about this, I appreciate how God has worked through other women in my life. When I was young and single, I became good friends with one of my co-teachers, Meredith, learning about teaching and life as she invited me to do things with her family. Marge taught me the importance of reading God's Word, showing me practical ways to listen and learn. God has blessed and multiplied the spiritual disciplines Marge taught me twenty-five years ago. From Lyn and Michelle, lifetime friends, I have become a better mom and wife, learning from their examples and talking through problems together. Here's my point: what would we miss if we didn't develop strong friendships?

The greatest gift we give to others is the invitation to simply be themselves, to be real, imperfect, quirky, and unique.

What keeps us from building relationships and inviting others *in*? Especially for introverts or women who've been wounded by friends, inviting is an act of courage. It can feel risky to put yourself out there, asking someone you don't know well to get together or to reveal something personal about yourself. A few months ago I met Andy at a church gathering. A very shy person, Andy almost didn't come, feeling awkward around a large group of women. As I talked with Andy, we connected on a heart level and I sensed God was working through our conversation. Hesitantly, Andy looked up and asked, "Would you be interested in getting together sometime?" Delighted with the invitation, I looked Andy in the eye and recognized her bravery was holy in the moment. For Andy, this simple invitation was a daring act of courage, and it was the beginning of a sweet relationship.

Invite others to be real. The greatest gift we give to others is the invitation to simply be themselves, to be real, imperfect, quirky, and unique. As women, we so often struggle with keeping up appearances. Relationships can be catty and competitive, with comparison being the name of a game with unspoken rules. Making judgments based on appearances prevents us from seeing the beauty of others. God has given us the gift of sisterhood to complement rather than compete with each other.

As we learn to recognize the tendencies and tender spots triggering our flesh, we make more and more choices to live out of our identity in Christ and rely on His Spirit in our friendships. I agree with Brené Brown when she writes, "Authenticity is the daily practice of letting go of who we think we're supposed to be and embracing who we are. . . . I can call courage, compassion and connection the gifts of imperfection. When we're willing to be imperfect and real, these gifts just keep giving."[1] Knowing we are fully accepted, loved, and valued in Jesus frees us from the pressure of getting it all together to impress and keep up with other people. Something magical happens when we give the gift of being imperfect to others as well as to ourselves. Even in the church, we struggle with image and perception. Our own honesty and transparency can encourage friends to be vulnerable as well. When we accept and appreciate others just as they are, we invite them *in*, creating a safe and sacred space for deep friendships.

Real friends are worth it. I've learned a lot about building community through the *gift of girlfriend* from my friend Larissa. Though we no longer live in the same town, distance has not changed a bond of friends who have become sisters. Recently we were talking about friendship, and Larissa commented: "Sometimes friends have irritating quirks. I have two friends that I love dearly, but they often run late. For me, tardiness is hard to handle—it frustrates me. I remember the day God showed me accepting others includes our imperfections. I decided they are worth it—the value of the friendship is more important than my preferences. I also have frustrating traits, and we've learned to embrace each other *as is*. These two gals are so WORTH IT! Now I plan a little extra time so I'm not stressed when they're late, and they make more effort to be on time."

Navigating problems in relationships can make it hard to choose holiness. Friendship between women isn't always an easy thing. My first lesson in this came in fourth grade. One day Jamie and I were best friends, and the next she was distant. It was my first experience of being unfriended in the game of who's cool and who's not. As adults, we can still be competitive and exclusive in friendships, never truly outgrowing the insecurity and clique mentality of middle school days. Relationships can be a flesh-fest when we are around this kind of person. Problems with gossip, exclusivity, and unkindness can tempt us to react with our flesh. If we aren't careful, it's easy to retaliate, criticize, complain, withdraw, blame, excuse, or compromise, with all kinds of feel-bad-about-ourselves thoughts. None of these is a holy choice or a pleasant experience.

Competition, comparison, and cliques aren't the only barriers to friendship. **A deeper challenge is being able to talk about problems in a relationship.** "I miss Angie so much," Jenny says with a sigh, leaning back in her chair. "I needed to set some boundaries in our friendship. Seems like I am always running to her rescue. I finally realized Angie was never available when I needed support. When I tried to talk about it, she was offended and upset. Now she hardly talks to me at all. This is really hard because our husbands work together, and we see them a lot."

Listening, my heart aches for both Angie and Jenny, for I know they've been friends for years. Jenny was brave to take the risk of trying to address a problem. As a tear slips down Jenny's cheek, I'm reminded friendship is a gift, not a given, for friendships don't always work out. Though this isn't what Jenny wants, I see holiness in her willingness to forgive and trust God in the midst of the problem. These are the painful moments when we need to choose holiness by examining our thoughts and feelings, surrendering our preferences, and forgiving friends who grieve our heart. Trust God and choose to rest in Christ if you are experiencing hard days when friends are no longer friendly.

SIMPLE WAYS TO BE A GOOD FRIEND

Aren't we all continuing to learn the art of friendship? As we live out everyday holiness in our relationships, God continues to teach us more about loving one another. Sometimes we can all use a few new ideas or reminders to continue to grow the *gift of girlfriend* in our lives. Could a few of these choices increase your capacity to create lots of holy moments to be a good friend?

1. Be an encourager. Develop the habit of cheering for others.

2. Never underestimate the power of laughter and silly fun.

3. Reciprocate. Good friendship is a two-way street.

4. Be reliable. Show up and value being on time.

5. Stop feeling guilty about spending time with friends. It is an important part of life and not just a luxury.

6. Be intentional. Don't let busyness crowd out friendship. The busier you are, the more important it is to plan ahead.

7. Refuse to gossip, and find a graceful way to squelch rumors when you hear them.

8. Keep confidences. When friends ask you not to repeat information, honor their requests.

9. Share the load. Help, listen, or console when it is needed.

10. Be real. Be brave about sharing your needs and struggles when appropriate.

11. Be patient as you decide your friend is more important than minor differences bothering you.

12. Give the gift of belonging. Welcome newcomers and include others. You may have a set group of friends, but be willing to make room for more.

13. Spark meaningful conversations by asking engaging questions. Small talk has a place, but sharing our heart stories builds relationships.

14. Don't monopolize conversations or only talk about yourself. Give the gift of a listening ear.

15. Avoid the trap of comparison and envy. Recognize these destructive thoughts and get rid of them.

16. Free yourself of expectations.

17. Be quick to give and ask for forgiveness. Treat others the way you want to be treated in this difficult area of relationships.

18. Let go of judgment and criticism; give others the benefit of the doubt. Assume good intention rather than immediately jumping to conclusions.

19. Be thankful. A cherished friend is a gift from God.

We may not be able to do all of these things at the same time or keep it up all the time, but we can all do some of these things more often. Treasure the joyful gift of friendship as you choose to be the friend you want to have, inviting others to grace-filled friendship.

Holiness makes a practical difference in our lives, and this includes our friendships. Friend, there's no better time to invite someone into a deeper friendship. Let the Holy Spirit be your guide, and you'll be surprised by what He can do through your friendships. And by the way, dinner's at six, so come on over!

SIMPLE REMINDERS TO BE A GOOD FRIEND

- Be the friend you want to have.
- When we *put on* the qualities of the Spirit, we are free to love our friends with open hearts.
- Every friendship begins with an invitation.
- Inviting friends over creates memorable moments.
- Invite friends in to a deeper relationship.
- Invite others to be real.
- Real friends are worth it.

CHAPTER 16

MOMENTS TO WORK

Good works are an overflow of our relationship with God, and
evidence of His life being expressed through us.

—Steve McVey, *Grace Walk*

Nervous, I walk into a room filled with writers. Four hundred people chatter
with the excited buzz of introductions and small talk. This is my first professional writer's conference, and I have to say it is a little intimidating. *After all,
I'm not a real writer,* I say to myself, opening the door for my Inner Wimp
(remember her?) to barge in. *You don't belong here. If you leave now, no one will
notice,* my Inner Wimp pulls out the *you're-an-imposter* lie. *Really, you're just a
volunteer....* I'm reminded of how easy it is to find our identities in what we
do rather than who we are. Self-doubt hinders our desire to cultivate our gifts
and talents.

Finding value and significance through our work and accomplishment is
epidemic in our culture. When someone asks me what I do, I'm not sure how
to answer because I *do* many different kinds of work. And I know you do too.
"Which job do you want to know about," I answer playfully. "My profession?
My current job? My work as a wife, mom, daughter, and friend? Or how about
my work in ministry? Or the daily work of keeping my home?" *No, let's not talk
about that one...*

God has a purpose in all the work you do—vocation, family, or ministry.
Whether you are the CEO of a corporation or Chief Inspirational Officer of
your family, holy moments are for doing the work God calls us to do. Friend,

your work includes the context of your *entire* life, not just the job you may or may not currently hold.

Brother Lawrence believed "simple work becomes the sacrament of the present moment."[1] In every kind of work, you are God's girl on the job, and your work matters. God has blessed you with a beautiful design made up of talents, skills, gifts, and personality. God has a purpose for your life, and holy work happens as we respond to God's call. Here's a sacred secret for your soul today: "For we are God's handiwork, created in Christ Jesus to do good works, which God prepared in advance for us to do" (Ephesians 2:10). Any discussion of holiness is incomplete without the inclusion of doing the work God has created us to do.

ARE YOU BUSY WITH YOUR PLANS OR GOD'S PURPOSE?

"Lord, please bless my work." We've all prayed some version of this prayer, haven't we? We seek blessing on our efforts as we serve God, but the New Testament model of Christianity is not to dedicate our own work to God, but rather to allow God Himself to do the work through a person totally yielded to Him.[2] **Holy moments are for relying on Christ to work through us in all we do.** As you build the habit of abiding with Christ, trust Him to remind you to do your work relying on His life in you.

Holiness shifts our perspectives from working for God to working with God.

God-honoring work gives its best but isn't posturing for perfection or personal gain. Heart-full and full of heart, this is the sacred work we offer to God as an expression of love. **We often draw stark lines, separating secular**

work from sacred, but holiness is found in how we work in any task.
"Whatever you do, do your work heartily, as for the Lord rather than for men"
(Colossians 3:23). In her research on meaningful work, Brené Brown con-
cludes that because God dwells within us, "sharing our gifts and talents with
the world is the most powerful source of connection with God."[3]

EXPERIENCING GOD IN OUR WORK

What about the days when your work isn't working? Maybe you've been
bypassed for a promotion, or you've just gotten another call from the teacher
about your child's poor behavior. The house looks like a bomb exploded, and
you just had an argument with your husband. Where is God on the days when
your best efforts don't seem to matter?

Consider how Simon experienced Christ after fishing all night and catching nothing. "It happened that while the crowd was pressing around Him and
listening to the word of God, He was standing by the lake of Gennesaret; and
He saw two boats lying at the edge of the lake; but the fishermen had gotten
out of them and were washing their nets" (Luke 5:1-2).

We've all had a day like this, right? Maybe your whole week has been like
this, and you're tired of it. Weariness goes deeper when you've cast months or
years of effort, hoping to pull in a catch to make your work successful. Casting
our nets, we invest time, heart, and effort into the tasks and people who are
important to us.

Have you come to the end of the day muttering, "All this work for nothing? What's the point?" It's easy to get discouraged when our effort seems to
have no result. Empty-handed, Simon has nothing to show for his labor. Jesus
approaches right in the midst of his weariness. "And He got into one of the
boats, which was Simon's, and asked him to put out a little way from the land.
And He sat down and began teaching the people from the boat" (Luke 5:3).

I'll let you in on a little secret: Jesus didn't *just happen* to get in Simon's boat.
God doesn't accidentally do *anything.* So there's no random coincidence when

Jesus works in our circumstances either. He is in it with us. He's present in your challenges and in the nitty-gritty efforts of daily life. How might remembering that Jesus is in the boat (dwelling) with you strengthen you in the things you do?

There's something else happening here. Do you see it? Simon's goal was catching fish, but Jesus was up to something different. Simon participates in the work Jesus is doing when Jesus gets in his boat. At this point, He simply asked Simon to row the boat. I don't know about you, but for me, seeing these truths was an aha moment.

Isn't it encouraging to realize Jesus didn't wait for Simon's most successful day to enter His boat? This divine encounter happened on a my-nets-are-empty day. Do you ever think God uses only the best Christians in His work? The ones who are so holy they don't seem to actually walk on the ground? Has the lie *I'm not good enough* kept you from believing God will use you?

How do we enter into the truth of this story that happened so long ago? Invite God to accomplish His purpose for you at this time, which may be different from your current goal.

What truth is here for you today?

Take time for a sacred conversation with God as you allow the Holy Spirit to show you truth to fill your empty net today. Invite Christ into your work, your family, your life, and especially into the work that may seem unsuccessful or unfinished.

A HOLY MOMENT FOR COURAGE TO TRY AGAIN

"When He had finished speaking, He said to Simon, 'Put out into the deep water and let down your nets for a catch'" (Luke 5:4).

Weary and discouraged in our work, we may have days when we need courage to try again. Faith to trust God strengthens when we row into the deep waters with Christ. Some fish will not be caught in the shallows, and some lessons cannot be learned in the easy victories of life. Some blessings come in the deep waters only after our own efforts and resources have failed. Is God simply waiting for us to realize that toiling in our own efforts will never bring the catch God desires to give?

How well I know this casting of my time, heart, and work into nets that appear to come up empty. My first writer's conference was part of a long journey. Over the years, I have pulled up many empty nets—blog posts few people read, rejected book proposals, promising opportunities that fizzled. I felt like I worked a job I didn't have. Empty net living is hard.

More important than vocational work is the effort we invest in our relationships. My marriage had some empty nets when my prayerful effort to improve our relationship resulted in more conflict. Parenting often involves long-term effort and consistency, which can be discouraging. I drained myself with burdens and responsibilities that weren't mine to bear. Beneath it all, I often felt an underlying discomfort in my own skin resulting from the pressure I placed on myself to prove my value and get it all right.

Has the lie of I'm not good enough kept you from believing God will use you?

At first glance, your challenges may look different, but we've all had our empty-net days. It takes faith, grit, and courage to resist the inner current compelling us to quit. If this is you today, Friend, make the sacred choice to try again. Don't give up.

Although it may seem Jesus is unaware of Simon's struggle, Jesus chooses this exact time to change Simon's life. What seemed like failure to Simon became a holy moment because of the presence and purpose of Christ. Answering Jesus, Simon replied, "Master, we worked hard all night and caught nothing, but I will do as You say and let down the nets" (Luke 5:5).

Did you know a definition for *let down* means "to loosen or relax"? For a gal who struggles with anxiety, this meaning resonated with me in a powerful way. Just as Simon let down his net, he also loosened his grip on his work in order to take Jesus at His word.

Is there anything discouraging you from continuing to cast your nets? Many times I've thought it would be so much easier to clean my nets, put everything away, and head home. Something inside wouldn't let me do it.

It's hard to envision a big catch when all we can see is an empty net. I sensed Christ was prompting me to have the courage simply to try again, without worrying about the results. Holy moments include surrendering our rights to fulfill our desires:

- To succeed in our goals.
- To have our effort pay off.
- To be admired for what we do.
- To be rewarded for our work.

What rights or expectations would you add to this list? Let me tell you now, surrendering your effort won't come easily. When we truly surrender our work to Christ, we release our desire for esteem and success, choosing to trust God with our needs, hopes, and dreams. What could happen if you offered your work to God, rather than pursuing your own plans and ambitions?

Don't let failure or lack of progress keep you from trying again. "Never let the sense of past failure defeat your next step," wrote Oswald Chambers.[4] Just maybe, your problem is really an opportunity. What if what He desires to do is so much bigger and better than what you're trying to make happen with your own effort? Does this change your perspective?

As you surrender your right to succeed, you can be brave and resilient because you've entrusted the results to God. Placing your work in God's hands frees you to enjoy the journey with Christ rather than stress and fret about the outcome you think you need.

Surrender isn't a cop-out kind of thinking born from laziness or inability. For me, impatience to get where I want to go makes me resist God's timing.

Learning to trust His pace as He leads me to a deeper relationship is a valuable lesson in growing in holiness.

Be willing to wait, to struggle.

Be willing to mess it up and do it wrong.

Be willing to try again.

Be willing to pull up an empty net or to let go of your net to follow where Jesus leads. Put your trust in Christ, confident He works through your entire story, even your empty-net days.

Surrender is a mind-set that transforms your work into holy ground, as you trust God to work in and through you.

This may sound nutty (we've already established the fact that I have my crazy moments), but I believed victory over fear and anxiety meant I would never experience those feelings again. As Christ reveals the depths of my heart, the power of the gospel, and my new identity, He continues to say, "Do not be afraid. Follow Me."

Victory doesn't come in the absence of the flesh but in how we respond when the old ways come knocking on the door. It's unrealistic to think any feeling of anxiety means I'm not walking in the Spirit. Now I understand I must choose to embrace what God says is true. Reckon it to be true by faith. Put it into practice, trusting God with both the outcome and my emotions. I have to be willing to do the work of rowing the boat when Jesus says, "Head for the deep and let down your net."

You see, I wanted to learn how to overcome anxiety and fear, but God wants to teach me how to live depending on Him in the midst of the feelings. For me, this *catch* makes a profound difference in my life.

Is God highlighting a right you've held close to your heart—something you feel you have to have in order to feel significant? Does the lie of *less than* or *not enough* drive you to prove your worth? Is there a level of pride or fear motivating your work or relationships? I know this sounds like a lot of nosey questions, but resist the temptation to skim over things that may feel uncomfortable to bring into the light.

What would it take for you to release your desires to God?

WILL YOU LET JESUS LEAD YOU TO THE DEPTHS OF HOLINESS?

Obedience opens the door for blessings beyond what we can imagine. When Jesus directs our work, He can show us where the fish are located—where or how to direct our energy and effort. At times, He works this way, for He knows what fish He is after and He knows where to catch them. "But I will do as you say"—words of obedience and surrender; these are the words leading to deeper waters of faith.

Our nothing can become a big something when Jesus is in it. Friend, what could happen if you mustered the courage to leave the shallows and venture into the deep with Jesus? Because here's the truth: this story is about far more than the work. And it's not just about the fish. Not really.

When the desire pulsing through our veins and motivating our work is riveted on the big catch, our lives will only be about the fish. "For the one who sows to his own flesh will from the flesh reap corruption, but the one who sows to the Spirit will from the Spirit reap eternal life. Let us not lose heart in doing good, for in due time we will reap if we do not grow weary" (Galatians 6:8-9).

Chasing the success of our own performance or proving our own righteousness isn't the path of holiness. Our biggest achievements will be only the things we've been able to accomplish with the efforts of our own hands. And day after day, we will hang onto our nets, casting our hearts for smaller visions, and fish is all we'll catch. If our lives are only about what we can accomplish with our own strategies, plans, and abilities, what will we miss? What will others miss?

Think what this means for you. Isn't your work about much more than the paycheck, the successful child, the clean home, the promotion, or the position? What purposes could God have for you through your work? How is He inviting you into the deep? Is He asking you to trust Him beyond what you see in your work? Your marriage or parenting? Your friendships? Or an area we haven't touched on in this book?

The story continues, "When they had done this, they enclosed a great quantity of fish, and their nets began to break; so they signaled to their partners in the other boat for them to come and help them. And they came and filled both of the boats, so that they began to sink" (Luke 5:4, 6-7).

Very rarely is it just about us. The fish are a big part of the story, just as prayers we pray, work we do, people we love, and dreams we dream are big parts of our story. When Jesus does deep work in our lives, the blessings overflow into the lives of other people. Christ has been directing this entire encounter, filling the boats of Simon and his partners. So many times I have read this familiar story, focusing on the work and the fish. I have often approached this story from the perspectives of God's provision and ability.

It's easy to be enamored with the big catch. I've done that. I've asked God to enter my boat, and I've trusted Him for results with work that seems fruitless. When I've come up with nothing, I've asked for Him to fill my nets. And I squint into the sun, scanning the empty horizon for the fish to come. It's easy to chase the big catch, longing for the big win, or the big answer. But there's more to the story. So very much more.

Holy moments are for experiencing the so-much-more God can accomplish through our lives. Beyond the task, the success, or the failure, it is never just about the work. Just as Jesus enters into our needs and frustrations, He involves Himself in our daily work as He meets our needs, fills us with His Spirit, and empowers our victories. In every area of your life, it is never just about the present circumstance. And when we venture into the deep with Jesus, it is definitely not about the fish. His purpose includes these blessings for your life:

Deeper work.

Deeper purpose.

Deeper relationship.

Deeper healing.

Deeper faith.

Deeper submission.

Deeper victory.

The catch itself wasn't nearly as important as what Jesus revealed about His divine power. It's the same for us—when we see more of Christ, we also see more of ourselves. "But when Simon Peter saw that, he fell down at Jesus' feet, saying, 'Go away from me Lord, for I am a sinful man!' For amazement had seized him and all his companions because of the catch of fish which they had taken; and so also were James and John, sons of Zebedee, who were partners with Simon" (Luke 5:8-10a).

As I row into the deep with Christ, He shows me more of my self—what I really believe, what I am relying on, why I struggle with my feelings. But He also shows me more of His divine nature within me. With each net of my old ways I lay down, there's a little less of me and more of Him.

Jesus gives these simple men a revelation of His power through doing something extraordinary in the middle of their ordinary work. *And right in the middle of the struggle.* Oh yes, friend, holy moments of surrender are for venturing into the deep with Jesus. Are you ready?

- You will learn more about your sins, but you will be amazed by the magnitude of His grace.
- He will profoundly change your work.
- He will teach you to work and live by faith and not by sight (2 Corinthians 5:7).
- You will discover the joy of working from your true identity.
- You will recognize the difference between working from your flesh and working in the Spirit.

- You will discover this truth through experience: "My grace is sufficient for you, for power is perfected in weakness" (2 Corinthians 12:9).
- You just might discover His plans are far bigger than you imagined.
- You will know for sure it *really* isn't about the fish.

Holiness empowers effort with the purpose and will of God flowing through what we do. "And Jesus said to Simon, 'Do not fear, from now on you will be catching men.' When they had brought their boats to land, they left everything and followed Him" (Luke 5:10b-11). As Jesus reveals His deity to the fishermen their lives are changed. They are not the same weary men who got into the boat earlier.

I love the way Jesus addresses their fears and emotions that hold them back, "Do not fear." He gives these simple men a new vision of His nature, along with a new identity and purpose. "From now on you will be catching men." Seeing more of Jesus gives us faith to leave our nets behind because God's work in our lives makes us brave and changes our purpose.

When we follow Christ beyond the shallows, He invites us to participate with Him in the greater work of God in the hearts of men.

My friend, think of all we've learned about holiness in our journey together. Holiness opens us to the deeper, completing sacred work of God in our lives. I promise you, there is not one empty net in your life void of meaning and purpose. God is for you (Romans 8:32), and He promises to work everything together for good for those who love Him and are called according to His purpose (Romans 8:28). If you give up, reel in your heart, and leave your nets on dry ground, what will you miss? Journey into to the deep with Christ and let Him fill your soul with overflowing revelation, courage, and purpose.

Holy moments are for more than simply catching fish or accomplishing the task. Will you let Jesus take you deeper into the life He has for you? He provides what we need to leave the old ways behind and follow Him more intimately. When we've been to the deep with Jesus, He calls us from pursuing things to investing in people—from our own attempts to meet our needs to the freehearted joy of attending to the needs of others.

Leave the shallows, Holy Girl. Cast aside the old ways that have kept you in the shallows of what you can accomplish in your flesh. One holy ambition for every moment and for every day of your precious life—enjoy the deeper life with Jesus. What are you waiting for? Dare to be holy.

This is your moment.

SIMPLE REMINDERS FOR YOUR WORK

- God has a purpose for your life, including what you do.
- Holiness shifts our perspective from working for God to working with God.
- He's present in your challenges and in the nitty-gritty efforts of daily life.
- Release your desire for esteem and success, choosing to trust God with your needs, hopes, and dreams.
- Placing your work in God's hands frees you to enjoy the journey with Christ.
- Put your trust in Christ, confident He works through your entire story, even your empty-net days.
- Victory doesn't come in the absence of the flesh but in how we respond when the old ways come knocking on the door.
- Don't allow the lie of *less than* or *not enough* drive you to question your worth.
- Our nothing can become a big something when Jesus is in it.
- When Jesus does deep work in our lives, the blessings overflow into the lives of other people.

YOUR HOLY LIFE

What difference does holiness make in your life? I hope you're discovering your own answers as you read this book.

Caterpillars push against the cocoon, but the struggle builds the strength to fly, creating the freedom to reach the heights. And it is the process of brokenness, surrendering our hearts completely to God, that releases the power of the Holy Spirit. As long as we're holding on, holding back, or holding in, we hinder the flow of the *zoe-life* of Christ in us.

Something sacred and utterly beautiful emerges as we discover how to live in our identity in Christ. It's called joy. And freedom. And an abundance of grace.

It's called holiness. And it's through choosing holy in the moment that sets us free to love God and savor life in the fullness of Christ. Love God with all your heart, soul, mind, and strength—with all you've got and all you are. Stay connected to His heart with holy motivation and keep choosing to rely on Christ. Remember you can trust God with your spiritual growth because He *is* in the process of putting you together, holy and whole—spirit, soul, and body. So be free. Be you. Be holy.

Go in the power of the Spirit, and moment by moment bring Him glory by choices you make.

- When difficulties threaten to derail your faith, make one holy choice to believe God is with you.
- When the world glitters and entices with all the pretty things, make one holy choice to love God with all your heart.

- When you feel alone and it's all on you, make one holy choice to abide in Christ and receive His life as your source.
- When you struggle and strive for control, make one holy choice to surrender.
- When you are weary from trying to do it all, make one holy choice to rest in the provision of God.
- When the needs of the day overwhelm, make one holy choice to pray.
- When your thoughts and feelings elevate perception, make one holy choice to embrace truth.
- When temptations beckon, make one holy choice to obey.
- When issues arise in your relationships, make one holy choice to forgive.

Holy hearts are humble lives where God is on the throne and Jesus is Lord over all—every moment, every choice, and every dream. *This* is holy in the moment.

My friend, this is the prayer of my heart for you:

May He grant you out of the riches of His glory, to be strengthened *and* spiritually energized with power through His Spirit in your inner self, [indwelling your innermost being and personality], so that Christ may dwell in your hearts through your faith. And may you, having been [deeply] rooted and [securely] grounded in love, be fully capable of comprehending with all the saints (God's people) the width and length and height and depth of His love [fully experiencing that amazing, endless love]; and [that you may come] to know [practically, through personal experience] the love of Christ which far surpasses [mere] knowledge [without experience], that you may be filled up [through-out your being] to all the fullness of God [so that you may have the richest experience of God's presence in your lives, completely filled and flooded with God Himself]. Now to Him who is able to [carry out His purpose and] do superabundantly more than all that we dare ask or think [infinitely beyond our greatest prayers, hopes, or dreams],

according to His power that is at work within us, to Him be the glory in
the church and in Christ Jesus throughout all generations forever and
ever. (Ephesians 3:16-21 AMP, emphasis added)

Celebrate the difference holiness makes as you practice simple ways to
love God and live in His truth. With each holy moment enjoy the life God
created for you, and let His life radiate through you into the darkness of this
hurting world. Because, Holy Girl, you were *made to shine!*

You were made to be holy.

It's *that* simple.

ACKNOWLEDGMENTS

To these I give my gratitude for the holy moments you shared:

To my husband—thank you for supporting and encouraging me through the years of this writing journey. I would have given up long ago if you had not encouraged me to seriously pursue this writing and speaking calling. You are an immeasurable joy and blessing in my life.

To my children—you have taught me more than you know and you fill my heart with delight. I'm so very proud of you, I am in awe of what God is doing in each of your lives. Thanks for letting me share some of your stories in this book.

To Marge Kimbell and in memory of Dick Kimbell—thank you for showing me how to follow Jesus, love my family, listen to God through the Scriptures, value Scripture memory, and teach others. The life of our family is forever changed through your loving discipleship.

To Brenda Pace—I'm grateful for your deep encouragement and friendship as you challenged me to pursue writing. You saw this calling before I did, and I'm glad to have had such a good friend in this journey.

To Mary Keely—thank you for taking the time to look through my work, helping me shape this first book beyond the original devotional idea even before you became my agent. You taught me invaluable lessons in our time together. May God bless your retirement with years of joyful times with family and friends. You have made a lasting impact on the kingdom of God through the many authors and books you have worked with.

To Rachelle Gardner—it is a joy to have the opportunity to work with you. Thank you for believing in me. Your expertise and encouragement are invaluable.

To my friends Larissa and Jenny—Thank you for the gift of girlfriend! You have been the best cheerleaders and companions in military and ministry life. Thanks for being willing to say yes, the day I asked you to help write a book in a month.

To Lorilee Scheviak, my counselor, editor, and friend—God has used your Spirit-led counsel to deeply impact my life. Thank you for the gift of your diligent and wise editing during the writing process, bringing your professional knowledge and skill to hone the content of this book.

To Tarra Green—thank you for the amazing teaching and mentoring through the Grace Ministries True Life Institute. The truths and concepts studied have shaped this book. God waited until the last day of instruction to reveal the contract for this first book, and I know that was by His divine design.

To Kori Yates and the extraordinary women on the Planting Roots: Strength to Thrive in Military Life ministry staff. Kori, having the opportunity to follow God in forming and launching this wonderful ministry for women in the military community has been an extraordinary experience. The encouragement, prayer, and support of our staff have been a valuable part of writing this book. Friends, thank you for sharing your stories in this book.

ACKNOWLEDGMENTS

To my loyal blog readers—I am grateful for your support, prayers, and encouragement.

To the team at Abingdon Press—Dawn Woods, Brenda Smotherman, and Susan Cornell—thank you for the opportunity to publish this book. Your hard work, talent, and professionalism have been a blessing.

1. MOMENTS TO BELIEVE

1. Jackie Banas, *Miracle in the Mirror: Success in Christ Esteem* (Yucca Valley, CA: Visionwriters International, 2006), 133.

2. Dallas Willard, quoted in John Ortberg, *Soul Keeping: Caring for the Most Important Part of You* (Grand Rapids, MI: Zondervan, 2014), 39.

2. MOMENTS TO CHOOSE

1. Bill Gilham, *Lifetime Guarantee: Making Your Christian Life Work and What to Do When It Doesn't* (Eugene, OR: Harvest House, 1993), 21.

4. MOMENTS TO ABIDE

1. John Ortberg, *Soul Keeping: Caring for the Most Important Part of You* (Grand Rapids, MI: Zondervan, 2014), 46.

2. A. B. Simpson, *Himself* pamphlet, p. 2.

3. Michael Wells, *Problems, God's Presence, and Prayer* (Littleton, CO: Abiding Life, 1993), Kindle edition.

5. MOMENTS TO SURRENDER

1. Strong's Concordance G5486, s.v. "charisma," Blue Letter Bible, www.blueletterbible.org/lang/lexicon/lexicon.cfm?Strongs=G5486&t=KJV.

6. MOMENTS TO REST

1. John Ortberg, *Soul Keeping: Caring for the Most Important Part of You* (Grand Rapids, MI: Zondervan, 2014), 134.

2. Ortberg, *Soul Keeping*, 134.

3. Mark Buchanan, *The Rest of God: Restoring Your Soul by Restoring Sabbath* (Nashville: W Publishing, 2006), 3.

4. Emily P. Freeman, *A Million Little Ways: Uncover the Art You Were Made to Live* (Grand Rapids, MI: Revell, 2013), 29.

7. MOMENTS TO PRAY

1. John Ortberg, *The Me I Want to Be: Becoming God's Best Version of You* (Grand Rapids: Zondervan, 2010), 135.

2. Bill Gaultiere, "Dallas Willard's Definitions," Soul Shepherding, May 28, 2013, www.soulshepherding.org/2013/05/dallas-willards-definitions/.

3. Brother Lawrence, *The Practice of the Presence of God* (San Bernardino: Popular Classics, 2012), 31.

4. Thomas Kelly, *Devotional Classics: Selected Readings for Individuals and Groups,* edited by Richard J. Foster and James Bryan Smith (New York: Harper One, 1993), 176.

5. Oswald Chambers, *My Utmost for His Highest* (Grand Rapids, MI: Oswald Chambers Publications, 1995), February 7 entry.

8. MOMENTS TO LISTEN TO GOD

1. Henry Blackaby, Richard Blackaby, and Claude King, *Experiencing God: Knowing and Doing the Will of God* (Nashville: LifeWay, 2007).

2. Ibid., 105.

3. Richard Foster, *Life with God: Reading the Bible for Spiritual Transformation* (New York: Harper One, 2008), 62.

9. MOMENTS TO THINK

1. John Ortberg, *The Me I Want to Be: Becoming God's Best Version of You* (Grand Rapids, MI: Zondervan, 2010), 93.

2. Dr. Caroline Leaf, *Switch on Your Brain: The Key to Peak Happiness, Thinking, and Health* (Grand Rapids, MI: Baker, 2013), 71.

3. Leaf, *Switch on Your Brain*, 76.

4. Dan Stone and David Gregory, *The Rest of the Gospel: When the Partial Gospel Has Worn You Out* (Corvallis, OR: One Press, 2000), 185.

10. MOMENTS TO FEEL

1. Peter Scazzero, *Emotionally Healthy Spirituality: Unleash a Revolution in Your Life in Christ* (Nashville: Thomas Nelson, 2006), 69, 71.

2. True Life Institute, lecture on Surrender and Brokenness, transcript, 5.

3. Holley Gerth: *You're Already Amazing: Embracing Who You Are, Becoming All God Created You to Be* (Grand Rapids, MI: Revell, 2012), 45.

4. Brené Brown, *The Gifts of Imperfection: Let Go of Who You Think You're Supposed to Be and Embrace Who You Are* (Center City, MN: Hazelden, 2010), 24.

11. MOMENTS TO OBEY

1. Henry and Richard Blackaby and Claude King, *Experiencing God: Knowing and Doing the Will of God* (Nashville: LifeWay, 2007), 75.

2. Strong's Concordance G5449, s.v. "physis," Blue Letter Bible, www
.blueletterbible.org/lang/lexicon/lexicon.cfm?Strongs=G5449&t=KJV.

3. Henry and Richard Blackaby and Claude King, *Experiencing God: Knowing and Doing the Will of God* (Nashville: LifeWay, 2007), 180–81.

4. Jennifer Kennedy Dean, *Live a Praying Life: Open Your Life to God's Power and Provision* (Birmingham: New Hope, 2010), 174.

5. Gary Chapman, *The 5 Love Languages: The Secret to Love that Lasts* (Chicago: Northfield, 2015), 37.

12. MOMENTS TO CHOOSE GOOD ATTITUDES

1. Eugene Peterson, quoted by Emily Freeman, *Simply Tuesday: Small-Moment Living in a Fast-Moving World* (Grand Rapids, MI: Revell, 2015), 47.

2. Oswald Chambers, *My Utmost for His Highest* (Grand Rapids, MI: Oswald Chambers Publications, 1995), entry May 27.

3. John Ortberg, *The Me I Want to Be: Becoming God's Best Version of You* (Grand Rapids: Zondervan, 2010), 21.

4. Interview with John Piper, "The Essential Warfare for Holiness," audio transcript, episode 13, Desiring God, January 26, 2013, www.desiringgod.org/interviews/the-essential-warfare-for-holiness.

5. "G. K. Chesterton Quotes," Christian Quotes, www.christianquotes.info/quotes-by-author/g-k-chesterton-quotes/#ixzz4YfoxG4iN.

15. MOMENTS TO BE A GOOD FRIEND

1. Brené Brown, *The Gifts of Imperfection: Let Go of Who You Think You're Supposed to Be and Embrace Who You Are* (Center City, MN: Hazelden, 2010), 12.

16. MOMENTS TO WORK

1. Richard Foster editorial comment, *Devotional Classics: Selected Readings for Individuals and Groups,* edited by Richard J. Foster and James Bryan Smith, (New York: Harper One div of HarperCollins, 1993) 375.

2. McVey, *Grace Walk,* 31.

3. Brené Brown, *The Gifts of Imperfection: Let Go of Who You Think You're Supposed to Be and Embrace Who You Are* (Center City, MN: Hazelden, 2010), 112.

4. Oswald Chambers, *My Utmost for His Highest* (Grand Rapids, MI: Oswald Chambers Publications, 1995), February 18.

Thanks for Reading this Book, Holy Girl!

Now that you've got your holy on, sign up for my newsletter at GingerHarrington.com to continue the journey. Join the community of Holy Moment Makers by using #HolyintheMoment on Instagram, Facebook, and Twitter. Share how God has strengthened and encouraged you by choosing holy in the moment. Together we can spread the joy to many through our stories and photos.

Please tell your friends how you've benefitted from this book and leave a positive review on Amazon, Barnes & Nobel, CBD, Good Reads, or other sites where books are sold. Together we are finding freedom and enjoying life one moment at a time.

Because you were made to shine!

Connect with Ginger
GingerHarrington.com
Facebook
Instagram
Pinterest
Twitter (@GingHarrington)

CPSIA information can be obtained
at www.ICGtesting.com
Printed in the USA
LVOW03s2241140318
569902LV00002B/2/P